London's
Shops

the world's emporium

D1635462

ENGLISH HERITAGE

Contents

Specialist Shops 18

Markets, Arcades & Malls 42

Department Stores

Fortnum & Mason, 181 Piccadilly
Harrods, Brompton Road, Knightsbridge
Selfridges, 400 Oxford Street
Liberty, Regent Street
Dickins & Jones, 224–44 Regent Street
Barkers, 63–97 Kensington High Street
Simpson, 203–6 Piccadilly
Peter Jones, Sloane Square
John Lewis, Oxford Street
Debenhams, 334–48 Oxford Street

Luxury & Designer Shops

Asprey & Garrard, 165–9 New Bond Street
Tessiers, 26 New Bond Street
Bentley & Skinner, 8 New Bond Street
J W Benson, Hunt & Roskell and Elizabeth Arden, 25 Old Bond Street
Tiffany & Co, 25 Old Bond Street
Thomas Goode, 17–22 South Audley Street, Mayfair
Partridge Fine Arts, 144–6 New Bond Street
Burberry, 21–3 New Bond Street
Gucci, 32–3 Old Bond Street
Harvie & Hudson, 97 Jermyn Street
Turnbull & Asser, 72 Jermyn Street
James Lock & Co, 6 St James's Street
John Lobb, 9 St James's Street
James Purdey & Sons, 57–8 South Audley Street, Mayfair

Food Shops & Grocery Stores

Berry Bros and Rudd, 3 St James's Street
R Twining & Co, 216 the Strand
Allen & Co, 117 Mount Street, Mayfair
W Plumb, 493 Hornsey Road, Islington
Paxton & Whitfield, 93 Jermyn Street
Charbonnel et Walker, 1 Royal Arcade
F Cooke, 41 Kingsland High Street, Hackney
James Knight of Mayfair Ltd, 8 Shepherd Market
L S Mash & Sons, 11 Atlantic Road, Brixton
J Evans, 35 Cleveland Street, Euston
Fruits of Paradise, 79 The Broadway, Southall
Kennedy's, 64–6 Deptford High Street, Deptford
Crackerjack Supermarket and Off-Licence, 56–64 Peckham High Street, Peckham
A Gold, 42 Brushfield Street, Spitalfields
Sainsbury's, Greenwich Peninsula Branch

Acknowledgements

Head of Publications & Design: Val Horsler
Design Direction: Mike Nawrocki
Design: Simon Borrough
Print Production: Elaine Pooke

Many thanks to the following people at all the shops we visited for their help and encouragement: Bobbi Amarjid, Carol Bamber, Aaron Begner, Nigel Berriman, Simon Berry, Caroline Broone, Joyce Brown, David Broone, Samantha Brown, Toby Brown, Cliff Cakeread, Anita Cogan, Jeremy Cole, Helen Coogan, Fred Cooke, Tim Cox, James Darwood, James Daunt, David at Carrs, Alison Driver, Mark Evans, Michael Fadda, Belinda Fisher, Sylvia Fletcher, Jim Gill, Pat Graham, Paul Greer, Nicola Griffin, Sarah Griffiths, Mr Harvey, Patrick Heard, Mr Heller, Brien Hobbs, John Hunter Lobb, Elzbieta Higgins, Hutch, Joseph Irish, Vicky Jones, Erica Johnston, Sally Kemp, Tamara Kern, Tony Keyho, Michael Kiy, Patrick Lamb, Paul Littlewood, John Matson, Fiona McLauchlan, Michael Mann, Robin Nathan, Peter Nichols, Bob O'Dwyer, Robert Palmer, Stephen Pavely, Richard Purdey, Tariq Rehman, Ian Reid, Arnold Rosen, Eva Saltman, Geoff Sams, Karen Scherer, Graham Simmonds, Mr Singh, Alethea Smuts-Muller, Graham Speed, Tom Surrey, Mr Swaddling, Takana Tanako, Dennis Taylor, Janet Taylor, Leonard Taylor, Ian Thomas, Safia Thomas, Sue Thorne, Brian Towers, Armando Vinci, Brent Walsh, Alannah Weston, Ernie Whitcomb, Greg Williams, Peter Wolf

Many thanks also to the following family, friends and colleagues for their help and input:
Jonathan Bailey, Sidney Barker, Tony Calladine, Nigel Corrie, Alan Cox, Colum Giles, Katherine D'Este-Hoare, Edward Draper-Stumm, Mary Galer, John Greenacombe, Heidi Heilbrunn, Peter Guillery, Richard Jones, Frank Kelsall, Susanne Larsen, Kathryn Morrison, NMR London, Cathy Philpotts, Elaine Pooke, Stephen Porter, Ann Robey, Mike Seaforth, Joanna Smith, Colin Thom, the Survey of London, Charles Walker, June Warrington,

Preface

London is one of the world's great cities, an international hub of travel, finance, and politics, linking the Americas with Europe, Asia, and Africa. In an age when shopping is increasingly viewed as the 'new culture', the favourite pastime of the developed world, London is also an internationally renowned shopping mecca, rivalling cities like New York and Paris. Tens of thousands of shops are spread across an area of over 600 square miles serving a population of over 7 million and as many as 25 million annual visitors. Harrods and Bond Street are as well known to tourists as Big Ben or St Paul's Cathedral, while businessmen from Tokyo to Hollywood dream of visiting the tailors of Savile Row. Shops that have been in business for 300 years stand side by side with modern favourites like Gap and Top Shop. From fishmongers and newsagents to sari shops and department stores, filled with goods and produce from around the globe, there is something to suit every budget and every taste. Such incredible variety and diversity make it fair to describe London as 'the world's emporium'.

But beyond their social and economic importance, there is another aspect of London's shops which is often overlooked – their value to the city through their architecture and their history. They are an inescapable part of London's rich heritage, offering as they do glimpses of how life was lived from the top to the bottom of society, and from centuries and decades ago right up to the present day. It is increasingly recognised that the historic environment is not just about the grand and the special, but is deeply rooted in the immediate world we live in – our streets, our homes, the familiar things which give us a sense of place. Shops are central to this perception, particularly when they have been around for a long time – when they can be recognised as part of our heritage because of their longevity, or the sheer age of the buildings they inhabit, or the historical value of the society they have always served.

In recognition of the value to the historic environment of shop buildings and the threat posed to them by regeneration and economic change, a national project was set up in 1998 to create a visual and descriptive record of English shop buildings, as well as an analytical study of the development of shop architecture from the medieval period to the present day. This work will be published in late 2003 in association with Yale University Press. But in order to celebrate the unique place that London occupies in the history and activity of shopping, we have decided to publish *London's Shops: the world's emporium* as a separate, complementary publication, focusing on the project's studies in London which included a photographic survey of the major shops of the West End undertaken between 1998 and 2002.

This is an attempt to provide the reader with just a taste of the vast array of shops to be found in the capital. In a rapidly changing market place, where shops are constantly being refitted or vanish altogether, this is a snapshot in time of London's shops as they appear at the beginning of the 21st century. Since the photographs were taken, some have already ceased to be used as retail premises or have been altered.

The shops are gathered into categories – speciality shops, arcades, markets and malls, department stores, luxury and designer shops, and food shops – and, with some forays further afield, concentrate on examples within the central area of London, particularly the West End. Shops were chosen for inclusion for their historical, architectural, and cultural interest, and reflect three centuries of London's shopping history up to the present day. While this book may only scratch the surface, we hope that it will inspire readers to look beyond the glittering displays and brand-name goods, and take a moment to consider the places and spaces in which they shop.

Introduction

Every day London's streets are full of people shopping. Londoners head to the shops during their lunch hours, in the evenings, on weekends and days off. They are invariably joined by day-trippers from the suburbs, and tourists. On Saturdays the pavements of the West End are almost impassable as vast throngs shuffle up and down the main thoroughfares. This has become such a feature of London life that one of the first things newcomers to the capital learn is that they enter Oxford Street on a Saturday at their peril! While some of this activity is driven by necessity – for essentials like food or clothes – shopping has come to be viewed as a form of amusement, a pleasurable pastime to fill the hours when not at work or at home. Shopping has become so popular that when done to excess it can become an addiction, and a pill is reportedly being produced to control the condition.[1] Surprisingly, this is not an entirely 20th-century phenomenon; the roots of London's love affair with shopping can be traced back to the 18th century, when the capital underwent a massive expansion.

London had been an important trading centre since its foundation by the Romans in AD 50, and over the centuries it has continued to be a powerful focal point for the nation, as the seat of government and the court. By the early 18th century three-quarters of the nation's trade passed through London, and it was the largest centre in Europe for international trade.[2] As the century progressed a burgeoning empire – with colonies in North America and the West Indies and trading posts in India and the East – ensured a steady flow of raw materials and luxury goods into London's warehouses. This influx of wealth and growth in trade attracted more and more people to the capital, which expanded in all directions. By 1750 London was the largest city in Europe and over the course of the century its population doubled, rising to around 900,000 by 1800.[3]

To Daniel Defoe, observing the metropolis in the 1720s, London seemed an insatiable beast, consuming all the country had to offer:

…this whole kingdom, as well as the people…and even the sea, in every part of it, are employ'd to furnish something, and I may add the best of everything, to supply the city of London with provisions; I mean by provisions, corn, flesh, fish, butter, cheese, salt, fewel, timber, &c. and cloths also; with every thing necessary for building, and furniture for their use, or for trades…[4]

While London's main thoroughfares had been lined with shops for centuries, to meet the demands of an increasingly cosmopolitan and fashion-conscious populace, the number and variety of shops increased as never before. R Campbell's *The London Tradesman. Being a Compendious View of All the Trades, Professions, Arts, both Liberal and Mechanic, now practised in the Cities of London and Westminster*, published in 1747, lists literally hundreds of trades and types of shops that were then to be found in the capital. As well as more traditional professions, such as butchers, drapers, and booksellers, there were many specialised and luxury trades, ranging from bird-cage makers and perfumers to snuff box makers and fan makers.[5] As the capital flourished and demand for luxury goods increased, the seeds of a modern consumer society were planted. To some, shopping had ceased to be merely a daily chore and was becoming a key feature in the social life of the metropolis.

For London society shopping was a delight. Caroline, Lady Holland, daughter of the 2nd Duke of Richmond, enjoyed searching for goods for herself and her sisters who lived in Dublin, where the latest books or fashions might not be available. Writing to her sister Emily, Duchess of Leinster, in October 1764, she asked her to 'Let me have any order you may have…as I don't at all dislike jaunting to town in a morning…at this time of the year, tho' I detest it in spring and summer; but in winter 'tis an exercise that agrees with me'.[6] Men also amused themselves with such excursions. James Boswell, in his *London Journal*, recounted a visit in 1762 to Mr Jefferys, 'sword-cutter to his Majesty', in the Strand, where he was offered credit based on his gentlemanly appearance.[7] Shopping for food and minor household goods could also be viewed as a pleasant diversion. The society gossip and diarist Lady Mary Coke left a detailed account of one such shopping expedition in 1768:

After dinner…I order'd my Coach, & Jane & I went in it as far as the Strand; There we got out & proceeded on foot to the Exeter Exchange, where I bought Two garden knives, Ld Anson's Voyage, & the last addition of Thomson's Works; left them in the shop & went farther up the Strand…went on to a seed Shop, where I bought two enormous Narcissus roots …from thence we walked to Temple bar, where at the great fishmonger's, I bought three whittings & some shrimps for my supper; left them in the shop & went up fleet street, but bought nothing; & observing the light decline apace, return'd back, calling at all the shops where I had made purchases, & carried them with me to the Coach…[8]

Fig1 View of the showrooms of Messrs Pellatt & Green, St Paul's Churchyard; engraving from Ackermann's *Repository of Arts*, 1809.

As this makes clear, looking in shops did not necessarily mean that one was obliged to buy. Casual browsing and window-shopping were accepted by merchants as part of the retail process.

Indeed, shopkeepers seemed happy to amuse and fawn over the customer, as this account from *The Female Tatler* (1709) makes clear:

> We went into a shop which had three partners: two were to flourish out their silks, and expatiate on their goodness; and the other's sole business was …to stand completely dressed at the door, bow to all coaches that pass by, and hand ladies out and in… 'This, madam, is wonderful charming. This madam, is so diverting a silk. This madam, my stars!… But this madam –ye Gods! Would I have 10,000 yards of it!' [9]

While deferential treatment added to the appeal of London's shops, it was their physical appearance that most impressed. Foreign visitors thought they outshone those of Paris, being larger and better lit. In 1765 one Frenchman observed that London's shops were '…all brilliant and gay, as well on account of the things sold in them, as the exact order in which they are kept; so that they make a most splendid show…' [10] Visiting the capital in 1786 from Germany, Sophie von la Roche described how 'Behind great glass windows absolutely everything one can think of is neatly, attractively displayed, and in such an abundance of choice as almost to make one greedy.' [11] Oxford Street impressed her with its street lamps, while 'the pavement, inlaid with flag-stones, can stand six people deep and allows one to gaze at the splendidly lit shop fronts in comfort.' [12]

Tradesmen made every effort to entice shoppers with stylish and elaborate displays of goods. In the 1760s, Josiah Wedgwood had begun mass-producing new types of pottery, like his famous Jasperware, which caught the imagination of the public. All too aware of the fickle nature of fashion, Wedgwood insisted that in his London showroom the space should be 'Elegant, extensive' and the displays were changed regularly to lure customers back again and again. Tables were set with dinner services 'in order to do the needfull with the Ladys in the neatest, genteelest, and best method' and Wedgwood advertised his royal and aristocratic patrons, naming ranges after them. [13] Other retailers followed his lead. By 1809, the showrooms of glassmen Messrs Pellatt & Green were noted for their grand table displays with additional pull-out drawer displays, while enormous chandeliers hung from the ceiling (Fig 1).

During the first decades of the 19th century, influenced by the fashion-crazed Prince Regent (later George IV), shopping continued to be an obsession with London society, reaching new levels of extravagance. One visitor to the capital in 1807 observed that there was 'a shop to every house, street after street, and mile after mile…' and was surprised how '…luxury here fills every head with caprice…and shops are become exhibitions of fashion.'[14] The Prince's colourful friend Beau Brummell, famed for his flamboyant dress-sense, could change the fortunes of a shopkeeper overnight by his patronage. The area of St James's, where Brummell's and the Prince Regent's favourite shops were situated, was a popular place for promenading. Bond Street, the north–south thoroughfare linking Oxford Street and Piccadilly, was lined with the finest shops. In the afternoon it acquired something of a party atmosphere with ladies and gentleman arriving by carriage, sedan chair, and on foot to look over the latest displays and one another:

> And now our Brothers Bond Street enter,
> Dear Street, of London's charms the centre,
> Dear Street! Where at a certain hour
> Man's follies bud forth into flower!
> Where the gay minor sighs for fashion…[15]

Known as Bond Street loungers, their love of promenading and lavish display would influence changes in shop architecture and design.

While customers may have been captivated by the displays of goods inside, the mid-18th-century shop was often relatively simple in design. Some might have columns or other decoration on the frontage, but for the most part the typical shopfront consisted of one or two display windows made up of small panes of crown glass, added onto the ground floor of an existing building (Fig 2). By the end of the century the shopfront was increasingly viewed as a distinct architectural entity, with pattern books offering a variety of styles and designs to choose from. In the Regency period advances in manufacturing techniques allowed a gradual introduction of larger panes of glass, and the shop exterior became increasingly elaborate. Society's love of the promenade seems to have led to one major advance in shop architecture – the arcade. Pioneered on the continent, one of Britain's first examples was the

Fig 2 18th-century shopfronts in Lambeth Palace Yard, c1883

Fig 3 Burlington Arcade, Piccadilly entrance; from *Metropolitan Improvements...*, by James Elmes, 1827

Fig 4 Interior of the Burlington Arcade, anonymous engraving c1830

Burlington Arcade, opened in 1819. Its elegant Piccadilly façade of columns and arches led into a top-lit passage lined on both sides with a variety of stylish little shops (Figs 3, 4). Offering fashionable shoppers a place to saunter and browse in inclement weather, Burlington Arcade was an instant success, and was soon being imitated elsewhere in London and in major provincial towns.

The Prince Regent inspired the creation of London's first purpose-built shopping boulevard, the most impressive piece of urban planning of the era. Named for him, Regent Street was designed by the Prince's favourite architect John Nash in

1819–23, with classical stuccoed façades and seemingly endless shop windows. Nash envisaged it as a grand thoroughfare where '...shops appropriated to articles of taste and fashion will...arrange themselves' and which would offer enough 'room for all the fashionable shops to be assembled in one Street...' (Fig 5).[16] It soon rivalled Bond Street as a place where 'between three and six o'clock every afternoon, celebrities jostle you at every step you take...'.[17] While the goods on sale in Regent Street were the height of fashion, within two decades its shop fronts were to seem plain and dull in comparison with those designed by the industrious and eclectic Victorians.

Fig 5 Regent Street, view of the north-east side; from *Metropolitan Improvements...*, by James Elmes, 1827

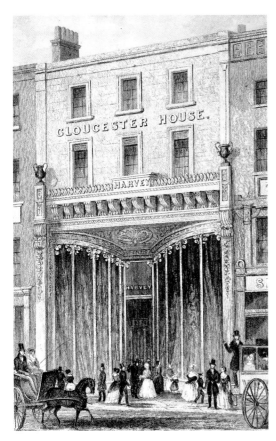

Fig 6 John Harvey & Co, Ludgate Hill, c1840

By the 1840s new technology and mass production were fuelling a complete metamorphosis of the London shop. The introduction of factory-produced plate-glass and cast-iron allowed for vast uninterrupted expanses of windows and larger, more open, internal spaces in shop buildings. The architectural detailing of shop exteriors also became more elaborate and varied. The Victorian love for revivalism resulted in Gothic, Renaissance, Egyptian, or Classical shopfronts, sometimes fancifully combined to astounding effect (Fig 6). To one eloquent commentator, writing in the 1860s, these 'palatial buildings – costly warehouses, filled with the treasures of the earth…' gave the impression that London's streets were '…bordered with gold, and bound on each side by glittering edges, as rich as the jewels and precious ornaments fringing the costliest robe that ever [a] monarch wore.'[18] The number and variety of shops matched the splendour of the architecture. Oxford Street was said to include everything '…from the most elegant drapers' shops down to the lowest oyster-stall…'[19] As the century progressed, émigré communities, notably the French, Italians, and Eastern European Jews, brought their talents, fashions, and food to the capital's streets. In 1857 one guidebook estimated that there were more than 23,000 tailors and 40,000 milliners and dressmakers in the capital.[20] Britain's vast colonial empire and her expanding manufacturing industries allowed London's shops to offer an unprecedented variety of goods – from exotic spices to mass-produced textiles – at prices that made them increasingly accessible to a larger audience.

Fig 7 Peter Robinson, Oxford Circus, c1900; the store had shop space along Oxford Street on both sides of Oxford Circus

Fig 8 Liberty & Co, Regent Street, c1910; the firm then had premises to the left and right of Maison Lewis in the centre

The rise of mass production, facilitated by inventions like the steam engine and automated spinning and weaving machinery developed in the late 18th and early 19th centuries, made possible the arrival of department stores. Many grew out of the drapers' shops that proliferated across the capital, benefiting from new and cheaper varieties of textiles, satins, and silks. Some concerns began putting set prices on the merchandise and insisting on cash payments, thereby keeping prices low and ensuring a swift turnover. Once a successful niche was established, new product lines were added to keep customers loyal and to remain competitive with neighbouring rivals. West End firms like Peter Robinson and Liberty followed this pattern, gradually absorbing adjoining buildings to create more selling space (Figs 7, 8). Others, like Whiteleys in Westbourne Grove, found their expansion facilitated by the development of the suburban railways and the Underground railway system from the 1860s onwards. These promoted the outward growth of London and allowed both out-of-town and West End shoppers to travel further afield.

The growth of these large emporiums caused apprehension among certain sections of society, who felt they allowed women to indulge in excess. One writer suggested in 1875 that in the 'mystical feminine meaning, to shop is to pass so many hours in a shop on the mere chance of buying something…[It] springs immediately from a taste for novel and various entertainment…[and] seems to be undertaken for the pure love of occupation.'[21] But however indulgent they seemed, London's department stores lacked the sophistication of those in Paris. There the first emporiums with goods arranged into different departments had emerged in the 1850s. By the early 1870s firms like the Bon Marché were rebuilding their premises on a grand scale with top-lit atriums and multiple floors. Although a department store named after the Bon Marché was erected in Brixton in the mid-1870s, it was not until the 1880s and 1890s that such purpose-built department store buildings became the norm in London and even then few matched the splendour and theatricality of those in Paris.

The success of the department store had been ensured by a burgeoning middle class whose desire for all manner of goods also influenced the rise of other types of shops. As row upon row of Victorian terrace houses sprouted in new areas of the capital and on its fringes, emporiums specialising in household goods, and large furniture stores like Heals, proliferated and thrived. Multiple retailers such as Boots and Marks & Spencer also began to appear. By the end of the first decade of the 20th century most local high streets were dotted with Marks & Spencer's penny bazaars and branches of other multiples, while brand names from Pear's Soap to Hovis bread also became prominent (Fig 9). The West End underwent a dramatic change with the arrival of Selfridges department store in 1909. Its steel-frame construction made possible vast expanses of floor space. With its American-style bargain basement, soda fountain, and rest areas, the building was marketed as 'A Pleasure – A Pastime – A Recreation', a place where shoppers could spend an entire day.[22]

Many London department stores were rebuilt after the First World War, and were also provided with cafes and restaurants, all intended to entice more customers through the doors and keep them shopping for longer. Many of these new buildings were built on an unprecedented scale, with grand Portland stone facades enriched with sculpture and bronze, a sign of how important shopping had become (Fig 10). Regent Street was also entirely rebuilt in the 1920s. The *Daily Mail* thought its massive stone frontages were more 'suited to the flashing bus and the rapid streams of polished motorcars than to the old-fashioned coach-and-four. It is part of changing London and changing England.'(Fig 11).[23]

Fig 9 Boots, Enfield Green, probably in the 1940s

Fig 10 Dickins & Jones, Regent Street, probably in the 1930s

After the Second World War, convenience took precedence over grandeur as big supermarket chains like Sainsbury's and Tesco began to supersede grocers and food shops in London's high streets. They offered everything under one roof and also introduced self-service shopping, allowing the shopper to browse the shelves at their leisure. This idea of one-stop shopping has found its ultimate form in the modern shopping centre. An American concept made possible by the dramatic growth of car ownership, the first examples began to be built in Britain in the mid-1960s. London was home to one of the first, Elephant and Castle, but it could never be a realistic option for the densely built-up central areas, where the variety of shops and departments stores made the shopping mall superfluous (Fig 12).

Fig 11 Regent Street, looking north, probably in the 1930s

Fig12 Elephant and Castle Shopping Centre, view of main entrance

Fig 13 Gucci, 32–3 Old Bond Street, detail of window display, 2000

Fig 14 Yesterday's Bread, Fouberts Place, near Carnaby Street

The construction of new shopping centres on the periphery of the capital – Brent Cross, Lakeside, and Bluewater – has often raised fears that shopping in London would suffer, but the later part of the 20th century has proved one of its brightest periods. Brand names of one form or another have come to dominate. Alongside classic names like Marks & Spencer, new fashion chains have proliferated. In the 1970s and 1980s Top Shop and Next brought cut-price cat-walk styles to the high street, since followed by foreign-owned rivals like Gap and Hennes & Mauritz. In the 1990s luxury brands, including Louis Vuitton, Ralph Lauren, Burberry, and Dolce & Gabbana, rose to prominence, taking over much of Bond Street and Knightsbridge (Fig 13). However, pockets of individuality have survived, ranging from Carnaby Street boutiques to the stylish shops of the Kings Road and the vibrant markets of Spitalfields and Portobello (Fig 14).

At the dawn of the 21st century, fashion seems to be as much of an obsession as it was to the Regency dandies, though it is now something that is open to everyone, not just an aristocratic elite. Novelty and fashion have also accelerated change like never before – historic department stores are being stripped out and refurbished, and new flagship stores with designer interiors seem to open every week in the West End, while small shops disappear (Fig 15). Somehow London manages to keep its uniqueness. Traditional firms with roots in the 18th century, like those to be found in St James's, continue to thrive, while London's diverse ethnic mix has helped to create exciting new enclaves that regenerate and enliven the shopping experience. Ultimately, it is this impressive variety and vitality that keep us all so enthralled with shopping – Londoners and visitors alike know there is no better way to tap into the intoxicating pulse of the city than enjoying the sights, sounds, and smells of her bustling shopping streets.

Fig 15 Selfridges, view of new escalators, 2000

1 BBC Breakfast News, 12 March 2002
2 George Rudé, *Hanoverian London 1714–1808*, London 1971, x–xii; Stephen Inwood, *A History of London*, London, 1998, 317–18
3 G E Mingay, *Georgian London*, London, 1975, 12; Rudé, 20
4 Rudé, 21
5 R Campbell, *The London Tradesman*, London, 1747, 33–40
6 Stella Tillyard, *Aristocrats Caroline, Emily, Louisa and Sarah Lennox 1740–1832*, London, 1994, 171
7 Frederick A Pottle (ed), *Boswell's London Journal 1762–3*, Edinburgh, 1991, 59–60
8 Lady Mary Coke, *The Letters and Journals of Lady Mary Coke, Volume II, 1767–1768*, Bath, 1970, 349–50
9 Mingay, 104
10 M Grosley (translated from the French by Thomas Nugent), *A Tour to London; or New Observations on England and its Inhabitants*, Volume 1, London, 1772, 35–6
11 Sophie von la Roche (translated from German by Clare Williams), *Sophie in London 1786*, London 1933, 87
12 Ibid, 114
13 Neil McKendrick, John Brewer and J H Plumb, *The Birth of a Consumer Society*, London 1982, 12, 118–19
14 Robert Southey (ed Jack Simmons), *Letters from England*, London, 1951, 50, 68–9
15 Jean Desebrock, *The Book of Bond Street Old and New*, London, 1978, 69
16 Hermione Hobhouse, *A History of Regent Street*, London, 1975, 33
17 Ibid, 10
18 Henry Mayhew (ed), *The Shops and Companies of London and the Trades and Manufactures of Great Britain*, volume I, London, 1865, 5
19 Max Schlesinger (English ed by Otto Wenckstern) *Saunterings in and about London*, London, 1853, 103
20 Peter Cunningham, *London in 1857*, London, 1857, x
21 Erika Diane Rappaport, *Shopping for Pleasure: Women in the Making of London's West End*, Princeton, 2000, 32
22 Rappaport, 164
23 Inwood, 742

Speciality Shops

London is renowned for its many specialist shops that produce or sell specific ranges of goods or concentrate on a particular niche in the market. Throughout the 18th and 19th centuries the variety of such shops impressed and astounded visitors. There were shopkeepers who specialised in everything from buttons and perfumery to stationery, millinery, and tobacco. While many small shops declined with the rise of larger emporiums and department stores, London's size has always ensured that specialist retailers had plenty of customers. Today some specialist shops, such as Waterstone's and HMV, have become major national chains. Others are intimate spaces promising personal service alongside handmade goods of the finest quality, reflecting a way of shopping that is increasingly under threat in the fast-paced, profit-conscious urban retail landscape. From handmade umbrellas and travel books to discount household goods, London has a specialist shop to please every interest, taste, and budget.

Floris, 89 Jermyn Street

Floris, Ms Elzbieta Higgins serving a customer

Floris was established in 1730, when Juan Famenias Floris set up as a barber and comb-maker in Jermyn Street. Homesick for the floral scents of his native Menorca, he began blending fragrant oils to create the first Floris fragrances. This fine shopfront, with brass nameplate on the stallboard, dates from the 19th century. The core of the building probably dates to the 1670s, including the cellars, where Floris products were handmade until the 1960s.

The atmosphere of the shop cannot have altered much in the last 150 years. The fine display cases of Spanish mahogany were purchased at the 1851 Great Exhibition. In the late Victorian period, when handling money was thought to be dirty, coins were scrubbed clean and notes pressed flat, and they were then presented to the customer on a velvet-covered mahogany change pad (centre). This tradition continues, although coins are no longer cleaned.

Floris, gift boxes

The classic Floris logo in navy and white decorates these artfully stacked boxes which are also emblazoned with gold royal warrants for HM the Queen and HRH the Prince of Wales. Floris have supplied the crown and held the royal warrant since 1820, when they were appointed ' Smooth Pointed Comb-makers' to George IV.

Floris, antique scent bottles and natural ingredients in the museum

Over the long history of the shop, the Floris family kept examples of their many products. These are now displayed in a museum in the back room of the shop. At one time there were more than 100 fragrances on offer, including some that were specially commissioned: Special 127, for example, was originally created for the Russian Prince Orloff in the 1890s. Other famous customers have included the dandy Beau Brummell, Mary Shelley, and Florence Nightingale. Jackie Onassis favoured the Sandlewood fragrance, and Nancy Reagan is reported to have ordered soaps for the White House after using them on a visit to Buckingham Palace. Floris fragrance No 89 was chosen by Ian Fleming as the favourite scent of super-spy 007, James Bond.

D R Harris, Ms Joyce Brown holding a bottle of 'Pick Me Up'

Possibly D R Harris's most famous product is the 'Pick Me Up' used as a hangover remedy. Customers can still come to the shop and order a quick shot of this tonic over the counter for £1.

D R Harris & Co, 29 St James's Street, shop interior and displays

Chemist to the late HM Queen Elizabeth, the Queen Mother, D R Harris has been a fixture of St James's since 1790 and is thought to be the oldest chemist shop in London. The original Mr Harris was an apothecary who, as well as selling lavender water and colognes, created potions and mixtures to treat the ailments suffered by the area's genteel inhabitants. The shop is lined with drawers that once held the ingredients for the preparation of medications, perfumes, and toiletries. Until the early 1980s the toiletry products were still made by hand and packaged on site. The present premises are the fifth the firm has had in the neighbourhood, and their fourth in St James's Street. The fine Victorian interior, with original mahogany display cabinets, was brought from former premises.

Taylor of Old Bond Street, detail of shaving brushes

A selection of the firm's shaving brushes, set out in regimental rows – a reminder of an age when, according to Taylor, 'no gentleman would be… without his shaving brush, even on safari'. Still fashioned by hand, most are made from badger hair. Its very fine quality is thought to produce the best soapy lather.

Taylor of Old Bond Street, 74 Jermyn Street

As the name suggests, this gentlemen's hairdressers and purveyor of toiletries traces its origins back to a shop in Old Bond Street opened by Jeremiah Taylor in September 1854. Jeremiah made popular hair and scalp treatments from botanical extracts. His son Ivan, who had trained as a chemist, continued to develop herbal preparations. A branch was opened in Jermyn Street in the 1930s. Today it is the company headquarters and still run by the family. A one-stop shop for the fashionable man's bathroom cabinet, it offers everything from combs and mirrors to vegetable soaps and old fashioned bowls of shaving cream. Some of the recipes for Taylor's herbal-based products date back almost 150 years, and scents such as sandalwood, lavender, and avocado waft through the interior.

James Smith & Sons, 53 New Oxford Street

Considering London's weather, this is possibly one of the most quintessentially English of its shops. James Smith & Sons is internationally renowned for the quality of the umbrellas that are handmade in the basement workshops. Established in 1830 in Foubert Street near Regent Street, the firm opened this branch in 1867. Although the Smith family no longer live above the shop, it is still run by their descendants. The shopfront, with its impressive glass panels, dates from the 1870s, but some of the glass has been restored. Although this area, near the British Museum, is not the busy shopping thoroughfare it once was, Europe's largest umbrella and walking stick shop remains popular with tourists and discerning customers alike.

James Smith & Sons, Mr Joseph Irish making an umbrella

After decades of perfecting his skills, Mr Irish can create an umbrella, minus the cover, in 25 minutes. First slots are cut into the stick in preparation for the springs, which are fashioned by hand. In the final stage of the process, the metal frame is attached and the umbrella tested. Finishing touches include silver bands and decorative handles crafted from coloured marble, silver, or wood.

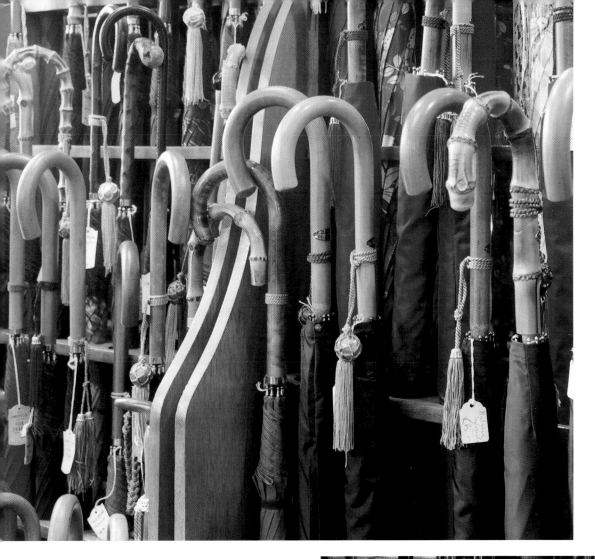

James Smith & Sons, a display of umbrellas

Resplendently arrayed with brightly coloured covers and tassels, the delicate elegance of these umbrellas and parasols is deceptive. They are far sturdier in construction than mass-produced models and won't turn inside out in the first heavy storm. Smith's use metal Fox frames, named after Samuel Fox of Stockbridge, Yorkshire, who created the first steel umbrella frame in 1848; before then umbrella frames were usually made of cane or bone.

James Smith & Sons, a display of walking sticks

This is an evocative reminder of a bygone era when all gentlemen carried walking sticks with beautifully designed handles. At one time these could be made with swords concealed in the shaft, but such James Bond-style trickery is no longer legal.

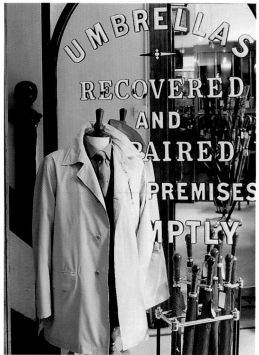

T Fox & Co, 118 London Wall, City of London

T Fox & Co (no relation to Fox frames) has been supplying city businessmen with elegant umbrellas since 1868. Their stylish black vitrolite and steel shopfront, accented with neon and prancing foxes, was added in the 1930s. Like Simpson of Piccadilly, Fox installed what was then the latest in shop window design, curved non-reflective glass, which is difficult to discern from a distance.

T Fox & Co, interior display

The interior, with fitted cabinets and panelling in oak and cherry, dates mostly from the 1930s refitting of the shop. Umbrellas were handmade and repaired on the premises for most of the shop's long history. This work is now undertaken by RJ Royal & Sons, makers of Fox Umbrellas, in their workshops in Sutton, Fox umbrellas can be found in major stores like Harrods and Selfridges and are exported around the world. They are popular in America, and the firm once made a special umbrella for President John F Kennedy.

G Swaddling, 21–3 Rushey Green, Lewisham

This family firm was founded in 1893, and has been trading on this site for almost 90 years. The first shop was the one on the right, with its stained glass lettered windows probably dating to the first decades of the 20th century. Swaddling expanded into the adjoining shop around 1937, and the large fascia, appropriately coloured 'baby blue', was added in the late 1940s.

Hamleys, 188–96 Regent Street, view of Pooh Corner

Hamleys was founded in 1760, when William Hamley opened a small toyshop, selling rag dolls and tin soldiers, in Holborn. In 1881 his grandsons opened a store in fashionable Regent Street, where the firm became legendary for the vast ranges of toys which have mesmerised generations of young Londoners. The business moved to its present premises in 1981. Spread over seven floors, it claims to be the largest toyshop in the world. Hamleys stocked the nurseries of the Queen and her children, and currently holds a royal warrant. Despite its fame, the firm suffered financial difficulties in the late 1990s. In 2000 a massive refurbishment of the store, including lavish displays like Pooh Corner (right), helped to restore its status as a legend.

C & S Discount Store, 109 The Broadway, Southall, Mr Bobbi Amarjid

Mr Amarjid and many other Southall shopkeepers use colour as an essential weapon in the battle for passing trade. Here a deep red canopy expands the shop space and invites shoppers in, while brightly coloured signage advertising bargain prices offers further enticement.

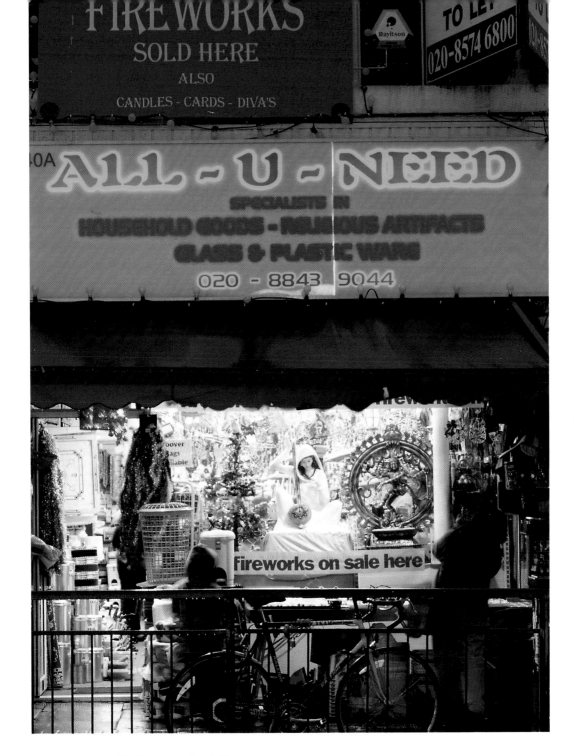

All-U-Need, 40a The Broadway, Southall

The shops of Southall have taken neon signage to new creative heights. The best time to visit is after dark, when the shops are brightly lit and the multi-coloured signs dazzle the eye. While this shop specialises in household goods, the window display illustrates that these can range from a statue of Shiva to a plastic laundry basket.

Robert Dyas, 19 Crown Passage, St James's

Robert Dyas opened his first shop in Fetter Lane, in the City (EC4), in 1872. Today the firm is one of Britain's largest hardware retailers, with over 60 stores nationwide. This quaint example nestles in a tiny alleyway opposite St James's Palace. The modern glass fascia, decorated with an old fashioned logo in gold leaf, was executed by Brighton signwriters W B Barden. It was copied from a historic photograph of the shop taken just after World War II.

HMV, 363 –7
Oxford Street

A favourite hangout of music lovers, HMV, then known as
The Gramophone Company, was officially opened by
composer Sir Edward Elgar on April 21, 1921. The name
HMV is an abbreviation of 'His Master's Voice', referring to
the logo of the dog and gramophone. The original store was
destroyed by fire in 1937. A new building, faced in alternating
strips of polished black granite and glass bricks, was designed
by Joseph Emberton and opened in 1939. On this site over
30 million records were sold before HMV closed in April
2000. Although 'The World's Most Famous Music Store' has
moved to larger premises opposite, this building continues in
retail use.

HMV, the spiral staircase

HMV's famous spiral staircase was part of Emberton's design
and one of the few original interior features to survive the
refurbishment of the 1980s. The neon and jazzy mirrored
panels, which produced the wonderful reflections seen
above, were added at that time. The staircase was taken out
after HMV moved in 2000.

Hatchards, 187 Piccadilly, c 1908, photograph by Bedford Lemere

Hatchards has had a long and colourful history. John Hatchard, having worked for various booksellers, set up on his own at 173 Piccadilly in 1797. He moved to larger premises nearby in 1801 and the firm has been on the same site ever since. In the early days Hatchards was both publisher and bookseller, and the shop also functioned as a meeting place – the Royal Horticultural Society was founded here in 1804. This photograph shows the back room in 1908, brightly lit by large windows. The atmosphere was more akin to an antiquarian library than a bookshop, with the more precious volumes kept in glass cabinets. Paired columns, oriental vases, and a leather armchair completed the scene. This interior was lost when the old shop was rebuilt in 1909.

Hatchards, first floor

An 18th-century style mantlepiece is decoratively used for an arrangement of books. Hatchards' clientele is a veritable Who's Who of the last 200 years, its customers ranging from the Duke of Wellington to Oscar Wilde and Jeffrey Archer. It has been the royal bookseller since its founding, when Queen Charlotte, wife of George III, was one of the first customers. Queen Victoria continued the tradition, and her son, later Edward VII, gave Hatchards responsibility for stocking his private library at Sandringham. The firm continues its royal connection today, and also stocks the libraries of the Houses of Parliament.

Daunt Books, 83-4 Marylebone High Street, the ground floor looking west

Nestled in the increasingly fashionable area of Marylebone, this bookshop stands out as one of London's gems. Described by the *Evening Standard* as an '…airy and elegant temple of travel and literature', its interior of stained glass, skylights, and oak galleries dates from the Edwardian period. Titles are uniquely arranged by country, and a wide range of subjects, ranging through biography, fiction, cookery, architecture and nature, are conveniently placed side-by-side with the travel guides.

Daunt Books, exterior view

The finely carved semi-arcaded front acts as a perfect foil for the shop's often thematic and imaginative window displays. The shopfront to the right is original; the entrance to the left was recently carved to match.

Foyles, 113–19 Charing Cross Road, ground floor, store directory

One of London's most famous bookshops, Foyles has been at the heart of the Charing Cross Road book trade since 1906. It was founded by William and Gilbert Foyle who began by selling textbooks. These are still a key feature of the business, but it is also world renowned for its medical department and antiquarian books. The ground-floor directory, which wraps around the stairwell and lifts, is essential reading in order to find your way around a veritable rabbit warren of departments spread over five floors.

Foyles, second floor, architecture department

Foyles' interiors have changed little in decades and are notorious for their quirky signage and haphazardly arranged shelves crammed to bursting point. However, this has not stopped the likes of George Bernard Shaw, Noel Coward, and Walt Disney from spending an enjoyable afternoon searching the stacks.

Foyles, second floor, the sheet music department

Foyles does not limit itself to books, but also carries an extensive music section. The seemingly endless boxes arranged by composer and also by instrument often turn up rare treasures and forgotten compositions.

Waterstone's, 203–6 Piccadilly, ground floor, travel department and Jermyn Street entrance

Waterstone's has become the UK's leading bookseller in less than 20 years. It was set up by Tim Waterstone, who opened a bookshop on Old Brompton Road in 1982. The business expanded rapidly, and was sold first to WH Smith in 1991, then merged with Dillons and HMV Media Group in 1998. The firm pioneered the introduction of coffee shops and cafes into bookstores and also made the move towards increasingly large branches. The opening in September 1999 of its flagship store in the Grade II* Simpson building in Piccadilly was the climax of this initiative. With 66,000 square feet of retail space and 1.5 million books spread over eight floors it is the largest bookshop in Europe. Included among its facilities are a restaurant, café, juice bar, internet stations, exhibition space, and personal shopping and wedding list departments. Most of the historic Simpson interiors have been retained in the refurbishment undertaken by building restorers Szerelmy Ltd. However a major addition to the existing fabric was this sweeping circular staircase and mezzanine floor above the Jermyn Street entrance, which provides a marvellous architectural setting for the travel and London book sections.

G Smith & Sons, 74 Charing Cross Road

Nestled among the multitudes of Charing Cross Road booksellers is this Victorian tobacconist and purveyor of snuff, a popular haunt of actors from nearby theatreland. The firm was established in 1869. The gilded-glass signage may date from the late 19th century.

G Smith & Sons,
displays of pipes

Lovely antique display cabinets, prints, and memorabilia give the interiors a unique charm. The original gas lamps (top right) are still in situ. The highlander was an emblem used by British tobacconist shops from the 18th century onwards. Such figures were traditionally placed in front of the shop.

James J Fox and Robert Lewis, 19 St James's Street

The firm of Robert Lewis, cigar merchants, was founded in London in 1787. J J Fox dates from 1881 and traces its roots back to Dublin. In 1992 J J Fox acquired Robert Lewis, bringing together two of the biggest names in the cigar trade. Two vintage statues representing American Indians and advertising classic cigar brands help to entice customers inside. While the highlander was an emblem employed by British tobacconists, those in America preferred the American Indian.

James J Fox and Robert Lewis, Mr Aaron Begner behind the counter

Here cigars are laid out in cases like fine jewels. The interior, with its mahogany fittings and comfy leather armchairs, gives off the relaxed atmosphere of a gentlemen's club. American tourists are often found here enjoying Cuban cigars (illegal in the USA), and famous clients have included the Duke of Windsor and Sir Winston Churchill.

James J Fox and Robert Lewis, memorabilia in the Freddie Fox Room Museum

The firm displays its archive of ledger books and memorabilia at the back of the ground-floor showrooms. Included among the objects are royal warrants, cigars from the 1851 Great Exhibition, a favourite humidor presented to the museum by the Duke of Windsor, and the leather chair that Sir Winston Churchill used on his visits to the shop.

James J Fox and Robert Lewis, the Manager, Mr Tim Cox, displaying a special humidor in the basement storeroom

The firm's stock is stored in a temperature- and humidity-controlled environment to keep it in optimum condition. Like fine wines, cigars improve with age, and some customers therefore buy the finest brands by the case. Clients, ranging from monarchs to movie stars, can store their purchases here, labelled with their name and date of purchase; their cigars are delivered to them as and when they are required.

Vinci Antiques, 27 Avery Row, near Bond Street, Mr Vinci in the doorway of his shop

Nestled in a quiet street near Bond Street is one of the area's most delightful characters. Mr Vinci has been selling art and antiques for decades, and has a story to go with every object. His window displays, with their jumble of treasures, hark back to Victorian times.

Witcomb Cycles, 25 Tanner Hill, Deptford, Mr Ernie
Witcomb in his shop

While the West End might be the crown jewel of London
shopping, the capital's vibrancy and richness owes a great
deal to the variety of local shops, like this bicycle shop in
Deptford. Mr Witcomb's premises, filled from floor to ceiling
with bicycle parts and paraphernalia, are situated in a historic
row of 17th-century timber houses that have been used as
shops since the early 19th century.

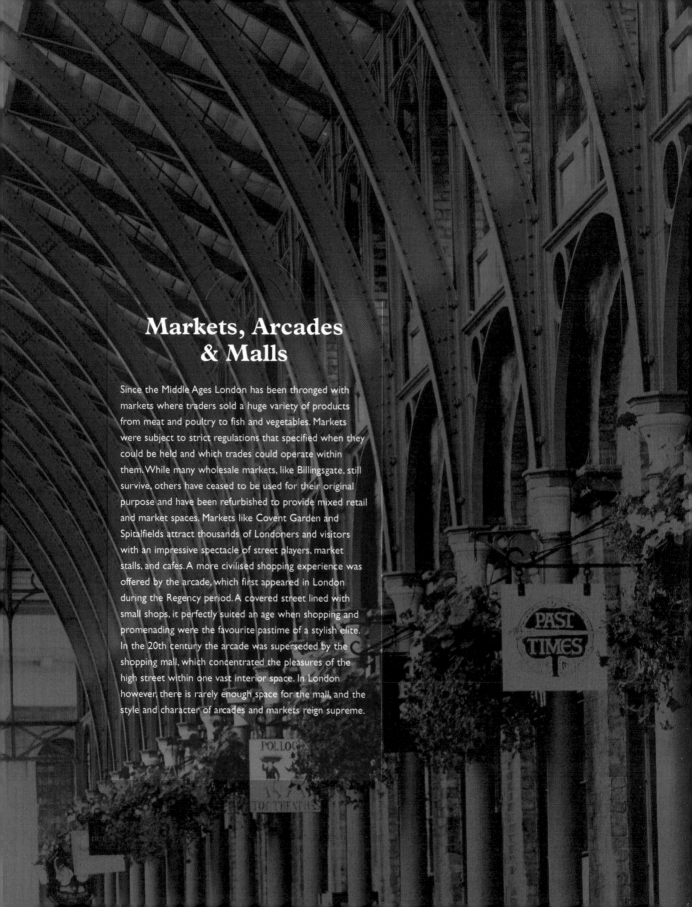

Markets, Arcades & Malls

Since the Middle Ages London has been thronged with markets where traders sold a huge variety of products from meat and poultry to fish and vegetables. Markets were subject to strict regulations that specified when they could be held and which trades could operate within them. While many wholesale markets, like Billingsgate, still survive, others have ceased to be used for their original purpose and have been refurbished to provide mixed retail and market spaces. Markets like Covent Garden and Spitalfields attract thousands of Londoners and visitors with an impressive spectacle of street players, market stalls, and cafes. A more civilised shopping experience was offered by the arcade, which first appeared in London during the Regency period. A covered street lined with small shops, it perfectly suited an age when shopping and promenading were the favourite pastime of a stylish elite. In the 20th century the arcade was superseded by the shopping mall, which concentrated the pleasures of the high street within one vast interior space. In London however, there is rarely enough space for the mall, and the style and character of arcades and markets reign supreme.

Leadenhall Market, looking east from the Gracechurch Street entrance

One of the city's few remaining markets, Leadenhall Market stands on the site of a Roman basilica. By the 13th century the basilica had been replaced by a lead-roofed mansion known as La Ledene Halle, and a market was recorded as taking place in its courtyard as early as 1321. In 1345 it was designated as a poultry market for traders from outside London, while Londoners sold their produce in Poultry, a street that still exists near the Mansion House. Eventually meat, hides, fish, and cheese were also sold here. The present market building, with its lofty glass and iron-vaulted roof, was designed by the City of London's architect, Sir Horace Jones, and built in 1881. Jones modelled his designs around the medieval street layout, creating long intersecting avenues lined with stalls. Originally these were all open-fronted, but most were glazed in the 1970s when poultry plucking was banned within the precincts. The original meat hooks (left), once straining under the weight of decorative displays of poultry and game, are now rarely used. Today Leadenhall is less a market than a shopping arcade, with stylish restaurants and shops having replaced many of the market's traditional traders.

H S Linwood & Sons, Leadenhall Market, Mr Peter Spence and Mr Joe Hanlon

In business since 1883, Linwood & Sons has had a stall here since the mid 1980s. It is one of the few shops in Leadenhall that is still open-fronted, and provides one of the most splendid displays of food to be found anywhere in the city.

Spitalfields Market, looking north-east

This is one of London's most colourful markets, with a rich history stretching back to London's ancient beginnings. During the Roman occupation it was a burial site; a magnificent 4th-century AD Roman lead coffin and limestone sarcophagus were uncovered to the west of the market buildings in 1999. It continued to be used for burials when the priory and hospital of St Mary Spital – from which the area takes its name – were founded here in 1197. A market was first established in 1682 when Charles II granted a charter for the selling of 'fish, fowl and roots' on Thursdays and Saturdays. The present brick buildings and iron- and glass-roofed hall were constructed between 1883 and 1893. The market was expanded to the west between 1926 and 1928, by which time it had

become a wholesale fruit and vegetable market. In 1991 this trade moved to new premises in Hackney and alternative uses for the buildings were considered, including proposals for their partial demolition to make way for an office block. While its fate was being decided, the market found new life as a space for sports facilities, cafes, shops, and the Sunday market, which has grown to include arts and crafts, organic produce, vintage clothes, and bric-a-brac. Despite the closure in 2001 of the western buildings, where a new office development is set to go ahead, the market continues to draw huge crowds and has helped to revitalise the surrounding neighbourhood.

Spitalfields Market, a stall with Miss Takana Tanako

Handmade crafts and artwork have become a popular feature of this market. Here Miss Tanako sells photographic-based works on behalf of an artist friend.

Spitalfields Market, fruit and vegetable stall

The brilliant colours of this organic fruit and vegetable stall are a reminder of the market's past, when such produce was its speciality. Today it is just one facet of an impressive mix of goods that draws up to 10,000 visitors on a Sunday. The iron-framed glazed roof, supported on ranks of widely-spaced columns, creates a lofty and well-lit space perfectly suited to such large numbers of shoppers.

Covent Garden Market

Once London's largest wholesale fruit and vegetable market, Covent Garden's beginnings date back to the 1650s when a few stalls started to appear on the south side of the piazza. Charles II granted a licence for a market in 1670. By the early 18th century the neighbourhood was home to scores of gaming houses and a favourite haunt of prostitutes. *Collins' Guide to London* for 1880 described the wholesale market as consisting of '…rows of shops …conveniently arranged for the display of the choicest fruits of the season…' and 'conservatories, in which every beauty of the flower-garden may be obtained, from the rare exotic to the simplest native flower.' This vibrant atmosphere was immortalised in the musical *My Fair Lady*, with the market forming the backdrop for the first meeting of Henry Higgins and the Cockney flower girl, Eliza Doolittle. Although the fruit, vegetable, and flower market moved to a new site in 1974, the original market buildings were revitalised with shops, restaurants, and bars, and there are still a few stalls selling antiques, crafts, and bric-a-brac. Today Covent Garden is one of London's most popular meeting-places, just as much a hive of activity as when it was piled high with potatoes and apples.

Covent Garden Market,
iron beams in the main
hall

In the 1820s modern market buildings were commissioned by the 6th Duke of Bedford and designed by Charles Fowler. Constructed of grey granite and yellow brick, the new market buildings cost the Duke around £61,000. The fine cast-iron pillars and arches carrying the partly glazed roof over one of the market halls, seen here, were added in two stages between 1874–5 and 1888–9.

Columbia Road Market, Bethnal Green, a plant stall

This Sunday flower and plant market has its origins in a grandiose scheme for a new market hall financed by Baroness Burdett-Coutts and opened in 1869. However, street sellers resisted a move to the new hall, and the building was closed down in 1874. Today, Columbia Road is one of London's most popular and colourful street markets. The narrow road is lined on both sides with stalls, and the friendly traders shout out special deals in an almost musical rhythm as customers shuffle by.

Columbia Road Market looking west, and detail of market stall

As well as the more typical plants and flowers, garden furniture, pottery, and antiques can now been found at Columbia Road. The mid-Victorian row houses have been restored and the proliferation of specialist shops and small cafes have given the area a greater vibrancy when the market is not in operation.

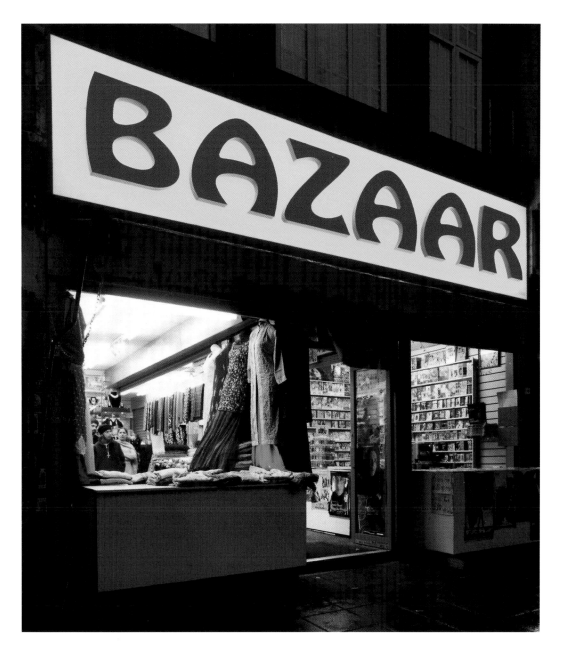

Palika Bazaar, 37 9 The Broadway, Southall

Many shops in Southall have been pared down to the bare essentials. Glazing is often absent to facilitate conversation between shopkeepers and passers-by. Colourful signage is also used to entice shoppers inside, and interiors are overwhelmed by the intricate display of products. The term bazaar may be old, but it aptly describes this type of retail unit, which consists of individual stalls.

Burlington Arcade, view from Burlington Gardens
entrance, looking south

In April 1815, Lord George Cavendish placed an announcement in *The Times* of plans for 'a covered passage with shops on each side' running along the west side of Burlington House from Piccadilly to Burlington Gardens. Lord George had seen the Passage des Panoramas on a visit to Paris and had been impressed by its financial success.

Legend has it that he was also annoyed with passers-by throwing rubbish over his garden wall, and decided to transform this derelict piece of land. His architect, Samuel Ware, spent almost three years formulating plans for what was a new building type for England. At 585 feet it is the longest arcade in Britain, and when built it consisted of a mixture of 72 single- and double-fronted shops with mezzanine storeys, crowned by a gabled roof with skylights. It opened on March 2, 1819 and proved an instant success, quickly becoming a favourite promenade of the fashionable elite. The north end was badly damaged during the Blitz, but the arcade was restored to its former glory in the 1950s.

Carrs of Sheffield, 22–3 Burlington Arcade

This historic silverware firm occupies one of the larger double-fronted shops employed by Ware to create a variety of projection and recession in this exceedingly long arcade. The first floor originally provided accommodation and storage space. The first-floor bay windows were described by H J B in *Burlington Arcade…*(1925) as looking like a 'quaint array of eighteenth-century opera boxes'.

Penfriend, 34 Burlington Arcade, window display and coloured quills

Although the shops in the arcade are quite shallow, the large windows allow for elaborate displays of merchandise, like these fine pens. Penfriend have had a shop here since 1991. The family of the chairman, Mr Peter Woolf, has been in the pen business since the early 1800s when an ancestor had a small business sharpening quills in government offices. The firm still sells turkey feather quills alongside modern pens, and has the world's largest pen restoring workshop near the Barbican.

Royal Arcade, 28 Old Bond Street, façade 1942, photograph by E J Mason

Opened in 1880, it was known as 'The Arcade' until 1882, when it was renamed to honour the many royal customers who patronised the shops here. These included Queen Victoria, who purchased riding habits from H W Brettel. The original nameplate survives on the central arched pediment, which contains a profile portrait of Queen Victoria. In the 1940s the façade seems not to have been brightly painted, as it is today. Like the nearby Burlington Arcade, it suffered bomb damage during World War II, but has been restored. The boarded-up windows of the florist (left) may have been the result of such bomb damage, although during the war shops also covered up windows to prevent damage and to protect against flying glass.

Royal Arcade, Albemarle Street entrance

The elaborate design, mixing classical relief panels, lions heads, and foliate cartouches, and crowned with majestic caryatids, was described as 'High Victorian Baroque' by historian Johann Friedrich Geist. The bright tangerine and white paint adds to the overall flamboyance. The granite lintel and pilasters are a later addition, replacing the original tripartite entrance which had four columns topped with urns.

A Maitland & Co Ltd,
1 Piccadilly Arcade

This arcade, which stands opposite Burlington Arcade, was designed by G. Thrale Jell and built 1909-10. It was not planned as a distinct entity, but as part of an office development. The curved windows of the shops at the entrance to the arcade, like this one of chemist A. Maitland & Co, act to pull shoppers inward. This fanciful display of natural sponges and toiletry items, framed by the frieze of fake seaweed and fish at the bottom, is one of the finest windows in Piccadilly. Its old fashioned style is once again becoming popular.

Reliance Arcade, Electric Lane, Brixton

The area around Brixton station is a hive of busy market buildings, shops, and open-air stalls. One of the most interesting buildings in this part of Brixton is the Reliance Arcade, which was built in 1925. The Electric Lane façade, decorated in a pseudo-Egyptian style, resembles the pylon of an ancient Egyptian temple. This style became particularly popular after the discovery of the tomb of King Tutankhamun in 1922.

Sicilian Avenue, Holborn

This street, essentially an uncovered shopping arcade with offices above, was built on the Duke of Bedford's estate between 1906 and 1910. Designed by Robert J Worley, it was part of the redevelopment of the area precipitated by the construction of Kingsway. A purpose-built pedestrian shopping street, open to the sky, was a new concept and extremely successful. Delicate Ionic screens mark each end of the street, while the bowed shop windows are flanked by giant columns. The façade and columns are covered with Doulton Carrara terracotta tiles. Originally called Vernon Arcade, the name was changed to Sicilian Avenue in 1909, a more fitting title for such a classical design.

Hay's Galleria, Southwark, looking towards the Thames

An excellent example of the possibilities of urban regeneration, Hay's Galleria was opened in 1987. The massive brick structure, designed by Sir William Cubitt in the 1850s, was originally constructed as warehouses with an enclosed dock, a final destination for tea clippers and cargo ships laden with exotic goods from every corner of the empire. By the 1980s London's thriving docks had vanished and plans for regenerating the area around London Bridge included the conversion of what was once described as the 'Larder of London' into a centre for shops, restaurants, and offices. The most impressive feature of the project was the barrel-vaulted glass roof carried on iron girders, which opens onto a promenade along the Thames. A 60-foot tall bronze sculpture with water jets by David Kemp, entitled *The Navigators,* stands at the centre of the plaza.

Whiteleys, Queensway entrance

William Whiteley was born near Leeds in 1831, the son of a corn factor. In 1851 he travelled to London to visit the Great Exhibition in Hyde Park and was supposedly so amazed by the vast array of items on display that he was inspired to create a retail emporium on a similar scale. He opened his first store in Westbourne Grove in March 1863, having considered that the increase in bus services and the opening of the Bishops Road station of the Metropolitan Railway made the area ripe for trade. Whiteley initially specialised in ribbons and fancy goods, but by the 1870s he was describing himself as 'The Universal Provider', selling everything from haberdashery to groceries and meat. However, this expansion angered local tradesmen, and in 1876 the area's butchers burnt an effigy of Whiteley on Guy Fawkes night. The store also suffered a series of mysterious fires and Whiteley himself met a tragic end, being shot dead outside his office in January 1907. The board of directors kept alive their founder's grand vision and had this fine Portland stone building erected along Queensway between 1908 and 1912. The use of massive columns recalls Selfridges, which eventually bought Whiteleys in 1927.

Whiteleys, the central atrium and staircase

By World War II the store was in decline, having lost trade to High Street Kensington and the West End. Its life as a department store ended in 1981, but the building survived to be completely refurbished as central London's largest shopping mall in 1989, with over 300,000 square feet of retail space, restaurants, and a multiplex cinema. Popular with local residents and tourists alike – the late Princess Diana and her sons were frequent visitors, often seen in the queue at the cinema – the new version of Whiteley's has breathed life into the area. This impressive domed atrium with staircase enhances a sense of grandeur and spaciousness that gives this shopping mall a distinctly American feel.

Elephant and Castle Shopping Centre, Southwark, looking north-east

London's first shopping mall, and possibly its least favourite, the Elephant and Castle Shopping Centre was part of a regeneration plan for the area in the 1960s. It was one of the first enclosed American-style malls to be built in Britain. Designed by Boissevain and Osmond, the three-storey shopping centre was opened in 1965. The box-like building, covered in textured fibreglass panels, dwarfed by the office block on its roof, and flanked on all sides by busy roads, has long been seen as a failure of 1960s inner-city planning. In 2000 a new scheme to rejuvenate this deprived area was approved and the present shopping centre will be demolished. A new shopping mall and leisure centre will be built around a pedestrian piazza, and the traffic that congests the area will be diverted under the complex. With the success of regeneration at nearby Bankside and Borough, there is hope that the £1.5 billion Elephant and Castle scheme will finally deliver on the promises of the 1960s.

Elephant and Castle Shopping Centre, the elephant

This statue of an elephant carrying a castle on its back marks the entrance to the present shopping mall. It has yet to be determined whether it will find a home in the future development.

London's Hair Fashions, Elephant and Castle Shopping Centre

One of the few 1960s shopfronts to survive in the centre, its restrained marble cladding is in sharp contrast to the bright signage of its modern neighbours

The Plaza, 120 Oxford Street, ground floor, view from the Oxford Street entrance

With so many department stores and famous high street brands in Oxford Street and Regent Street, the West End is not the place one would expect to find a shopping mall. The Plaza is one such rarity. From 1902 to 1983 the site was home to the department store Bourne & Hollingsworth. After its closure the building was redeveloped, and in 1986 opened as a shopping mall with four floors of retail space. The Plaza was not initially successful, but its stature has risen since a new refurbishment of the interiors was undertaken by The Colman Partnership between 1995 and 1996. Their creative use of an oval shape, enhanced by the illuminated glass ceiling, has dramatically improved the flow of shoppers from Oxford Street through the mall.

Department Stores

From the late 18th century London was famed for its
large emporiums and warehouses offering a variety of
goods under one roof. However, it was not until the 19th
century that most of London's famous department stores
were founded. Some, like Dickins & Jones and John Lewis,
grew out of small drapers' shops that gradually expanded
their ranges to cater to a growing middle class eager to
consume all the fancy goods and new products made
available by the growth of manufacturing. Others made
their name supplying provisions and groceries: Harrods
and Fortnum & Mason are still well known for their food
halls. However, London's department stores lagged behind
the grandeur of those emerging in Paris in the 1870s. It
was not until the 1880s and 1890s that the first purpose-
built department store buildings began to appear, and
there is now no doubt that the vast shopping palaces we
see today are among the most famous in the world.

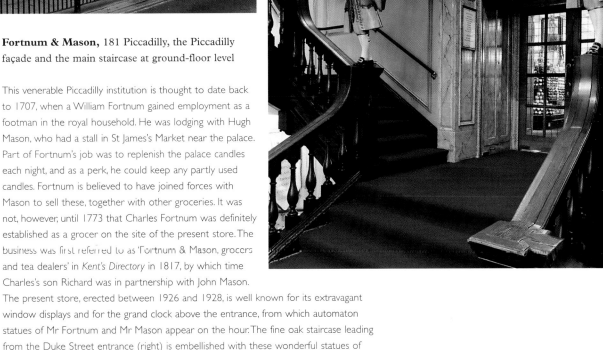

Fortnum & Mason, 181 Piccadilly, the Piccadilly façade and the main staircase at ground-floor level

This venerable Piccadilly institution is thought to date back to 1707, when a William Fortnum gained employment as a footman in the royal household. He was lodging with Hugh Mason, who had a stall in St James's Market near the palace. Part of Fortnum's job was to replenish the palace candles each night, and as a perk, he could keep any partly used candles. Fortnum is believed to have joined forces with Mason to sell these, together with other groceries. It was not, however, until 1773 that Charles Fortnum was definitely established as a grocer on the site of the present store. The business was first referred to as 'Fortnum & Mason, grocers and tea dealers' in *Kent's Directory* in 1817, by which time Charles's son Richard was in partnership with John Mason.

The present store, erected between 1926 and 1928, is well known for its extravagant window displays and for the grand clock above the entrance, from which automaton statues of Mr Fortnum and Mr Mason appear on the hour. The fine oak staircase leading from the Duke Street entrance (right) is embellished with these wonderful statues of footmen in 18th-century livery holding candelabra, an amusing allusion to the legend of the first Mr Fortnum.

Fortnum & Mason, ground floor, food hall

Displays of Fortnum's own branded goods and the finest selection of provisions from around the globe are set out elegantly in the ground-floor food hall. Fortnum's was renowned from the late 18th century for its 'potted foods' and exotic goods; many of their imported items were obtained through the East India Company. Cases of provisions were shipped to Wellington's officers during the Napoleonic Wars, and Queen Victoria famously ordered a consignment of concentrated beef tea to be sent to Florence Nightingale in the Crimea. There was a department responsible for sending supplies to famous London clubs like Boodles and the Athenaeum, and the provisioning of safaris and expeditions, including that of Scott to the Antarctic, was also a speciality. Although today the store sells an assortment of goods from stationery and clothes to toys and china, it is still world famous for its groceries – the firm holds royal warrants as grocers to both the Queen and the Prince of Wales.

Fortnum & Mason, a selection of hampers

The origins of Fortnum's famous hampers appear to date to 1788, when the store began offering 'concentrated lunches' consisting of game pies, lobster, and boned chicken for shooting parties and busy Members of Parliament. However, it was the 1851 Great Exhibition that made the hampers famous, with customers ordering picnic baskets of 'ready to eat' food to enjoy at the event. The concept soon caught on for other events like Cowes, the Derby, and Henley Regatta, where the hampers are still in evidence.

Harrods, Brompton Road, Knightsbridge

Harrods is arguably the most famous store in the world and a major tourist attraction. Its beginnings date back to 1853 when the grocer and tea-dealer, Charles Henry Harrod, moved from premises in Stepney to a small shop on the Brompton Road. In the early 1860s, Charles Digby Harrod took over the running of the store from his father. He attracted new business by offering free delivery, and kept prices low by refusing credit and insisting on cash payments. Increased profits, particularly from tea, allowed for expansion into new departments and the business gradually took over adjoining shops in Brompton Road. By the early 1890s Harrods controlled or had agreed to acquire the majority of the present 4-acre site and began to plan a massive new building. The store that we see today was constructed in phases between 1894 and 1912. The façade is faced with Doulton terracotta and is lit up by over 11,000 lights. It was designed by C W Stephens, who was also responsible for the equally famous Claridge's Hotel.

Harrods, Ladies Blouse Department, 1919, photograph by Bedford Lemere

Harrods, ground floor, Mr Jihad Houliet in the Tea, Coffee, Chocolate, and Patisserie Hall

Harrods, ground floor, view of the Meat, Fish, and Poultry Hall

Since its beginnings the Harrods name has always been associated with groceries and provisions, and it is not surprising that its food halls, arranged in 18 different departments, take up a large portion of the ground floor. The Meat Hall was built in 1902–3 and decorated with Doulton tiles. In 1906, Joseph Appel, manager of the Philadelphia department store Wanamaker's, described it as 'the most magnificent [room] in the store and handsomely painted with large designs and figures'. These scenes, including plaques of birds and fish, as well as the stylised trees and hunting scenes around the former lightwell, were designed for Doulton by W J Neatby.

This hall, built in 1903, was originally the site of the flowers, fruit, and vegetable hall and by the 1920s had become the bakery. More than 110 tons of chocolate are sold here each year, as well as 112 varieties of tea. It retains its original plasterwork ceiling and colourful Doulton tiles.

Harrods, ground floor, sculpture in the Meat, Poultry, and Fish Hall

This delightful sculpture of mermaids and seashells is adorned each day with a central decoration made from fresh seafood.

Harrods, ground floor,
the Egyptian Hall

Possibly Mohamed Al Fayed's most ambitious project at Harrods has been the creation in 1991 of the Egyptian Hall. Inspired by Mr Al Fayed's birthplace, designer William Mitchell fused archaeology and exuberance to create one of the most stunning store interiors in the world. The painted ceiling and many of the wall reliefs are copied from ancient temples and tombs.

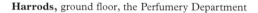

Harrods, ground floor, the Perfumery Department

In 1985 Mohamed Al Fayed purchased the House of Fraser group, which included Harrods, for £615 million. Soon after, he began a remodelling of the store which has so far cost around £300 million. Harrods' historic interiors have been restored, and new lavish decoration added throughout. The Perfumery Department, fitted out in black granite and enhanced with delicate art nouveau style etched glass panels, was created in 1989.

Harrods, basement, memorial to Princess Diana and Dodi Al Fayed

It is not unusual for department stores to have memorials to staff members who have fallen in battle, but this is possibly the first memorial to famous people in a London store. It was also the first monument erected in memory of 'the People's Princess' and her close friend Dodi Al Fayed, the son of Harrods' owner. Visitors often leave flowers and write in books of condolence, and on the anniversary of their deaths a similar memorial is placed in the main display windows of the Egyptian Hall.

Harrods, first floor, the stained glass ceiling and sculpture in the Egyptian Escalator Hall

The central escalator hall replaced the 1920s lifts. Built in 1997 in the same lavish style as the Egyptian Hall, it cost an astounding £20 million. The stained glass ceiling panel of a marsh hunting scene was probably based on paintings from an 18th dynasty tomb which are now in the British Museum.

Selfridges, Oxford Street and Duke Street corner, 1909, photograph by Bedford Lemere

While London's department stores often grew from modest beginnings, Selfridges was intended to be a retail palace in the American style from its inception. It was the singular vision of the American Henry Gordon Selfridge, who had made his fortune at the Chicago department store, Marshall Field. The classical Portland stone exterior, articulated by monumental Ionic columns, hid an innovative steel-frame structure which allowed the first section of the building, shown above, to be erected in just 10 months. It opened for business on March 15, 1909. The eight floors offered six acres of retail space, including a restaurant, an American-style Soda Fountain, foreign-themed rest areas, and 130 separate departments. It was a new and exciting experience for London's shoppers, and was described by the *Daily News* as 'a city epitomised — a compact concentration of the most attractive shops, of all the comforts and conveniences of modern life open to everyone…'.

Selfridges, detail of main Oxford Street entrance with clock and sculpture of The Queen of Time

The central block of the Oxford Street façade was completed in 1928. A decade before, Selfridge had envisaged crowning the central block with a massive dome or tower over 400 feet high, and the foundations were constructed accordingly. This grandiose scheme was eventually dropped, and the entrance was completed with this 14-ton bronze and Portland stone sculpture and clock. Enriched with gilding and blue faience mosaic, *The Queen of Time* was designed by Gilbert Bayes and A D Millar, and erected in October 1931. This photograph shows the figures before they were restored and re-gilded in 2000.

Selfridges, detail, main entrance revolving doors

The intricate bronze decoration on the handrail of the revolving doors at the main Oxford Street entrance is part of the original decorative scheme from the 1920s.

Selfridges, the central escalators at second floor level and the Espresso Counter in the Men's Fashion department, first floor

Chief Executive Vittorio Radice has been reinventing the store with a multi-million pound refurbishment. A new central atrium has been added, promoting a sense of procession and exhibition which complements the many new fashion departments. New eating and drinking areas have also been placed around the store and the progressive spirit of Gordon Selfridge seems to have been revived.

Selfridges, the Oxford Street façade in 1937 and 2000

Selfridges has a tradition of decorating its exterior in lavish and innovative ways. The photograph on the left shows the façade decorated for the coronation of George VI in 1937. Based on the theme of empire, the decorations included panels illustrating major events in British history, with sculptural ensembles symbolising the different nations of the empire placed at the corners of the building. When the façade was due to be cleaned in the spring of 2000, Selfridges decided to wrap the necessary scaffolding in the world's largest art installation, a 60-feet high and 900-feet long colour photograph. Commissioned from the artist Sam Taylor-Wood, the work was an amalgamation of portraits of personalities from the British arts, fashion and music scene, including Elton John, Richard E Grant, and Jodie Kidd. The work was unveiled in May 2000 and remained in place for six months until work on the Portland stone front was completed.

Liberty, Regent Street, main entrance in Great Marlborough Street

In 1862, Arthur Lasenby Liberty took a position with Farmer & Rogers of Regent Street, oriental goods merchants. He opened his own shop at 218a Regent Street in 1875, where his deep interest in oriental decorative arts influenced the selection of fabrics and goods for sale, many of which were imported from the East. The new business soon became known for its own fabric designs. Furniture, silver, and decorative objects were also produced to the highest standards of craftsmanship, with designs greatly influenced by the Arts and Crafts and Art Nouveau movements of the 1880s and 1890s. The objects created during that period are still highly collectable. The store continues to be admired today for its emphasis on design and quality. After a period of uncertainty, the building underwent a revamp culminating in the refurbishment of the Regent Street block in 2002. The Tudor block, shown below, is one of London's best-loved monuments. Embellished with teak, carved panels, and stained glass, it was designed by Edwin T and E Stanley Hall and built 1922–4.

Liberty, the east atrium

The interior of Liberty's Tudor building was designed around three light wells which provided views of the many departments and created places to drape fabrics and carpets for enhanced decorative effect. The oak panelling and beams are made of wood salvaged from two of the last wooden naval ships, the HMS Hindustan and HMS Impregnable, which were broken up in 1921. The painting of the ships is on display in the store.

HMS Hindustan and HMS Impregnable at Plymouth in 1860, painted by Leslie A Wilcox

Liberty, third floor, the carpet department and elephant carving around the central atrium

The interiors are enriched with decorative panels and amusing carvings of animals, like this marvellous seated elephant. This unique quirkiness makes Liberty one of London's most interesting buildings. The displays of unusual carpets and textiles from Iran, India, and elsewhere are in keeping with Arthur Lasenby Liberty's love of all things eastern.

Dickins & Jones, 224–44 Regent Street; Hutch the doorman waits to greet shoppers at the main entrance

Thomas Dickins and William Smith opened a linen draper's shop at 54 Oxford Street in 1803. The firm moved to Regent Street in 1835, where the business steadily expanded. After Thomas Dickins' death in 1856, his sons entered into a partnership with John Pritchard Jones, and the shop became known as Dickins & Jones. Although the firm continued to concentrate on linen and drapery, by the 1890s it sold everything from umbrellas and giftware to wedding trousseaux and enjoyed the custom of the Princess of Wales and foreign royalty. In 1914 Harrods bought a controlling interest in the firm and the present Portland stone building was erected from 1920 to the designs of Sir Henry Tanner. Dickins & Jones became part of the House of Fraser group in 1959, though it continues to retain its identity, here exemplified by Hutch, who greets shoppers with great style and panache.

Dickins & Jones, the circular atrium and escalators

Dickins & Jones has undergone numerous refurbishments since the late 1940s and the original interiors have disappeared. The elegant circular atrium was the result of one such remodelling and is one of the finest architectural features of the store.

Barkers, 63-97 Kensington
High Street, general view
looking east

John Barker was the son of a Kent brewer who, like
William Whiteley before him, was drawn to London in
search of his fortune. He arrived in the capital in 1858, and
by the 1860s was working at Whiteley's emporium in
Westbourne Grove, where he eventually became a much
valued manager. He left in 1870 to set up his own draper's
shop at 91 and 93 Kensington High Street, living with his
family above the premises. Within a decade he had
expanded into 15 adjoining shops, and by 1895 had more

than 60 departments and 1500 staff. John Barker died in
1914, but it was not until 1927 that his firm finally
controlled the entire Kensington High Street block and
could rebuild on a grand scale. The present steel-framed
building, with its stone facing and sharp vertical staircase
towers, dominates the area and is a fitting monument to the
vision of its founder. It was designed by Barkers' in-house
architect, Bernard George, and built in three phases
between 1927 and 1958.

Simpson, 203–6 Piccadilly

Simpson, which opened on April 29, 1936, did not begin as a typical department store, but as a men's store. In 1932, Alexander Simpson had created the DAKS trademark for the newest product of his family's wholesale men's clothing business – a new type of trousers with a self-supporting waistband. They were such a success that Alexander decided to open a retail store. Hoping to challenge the pre-eminence of Savile Row and Austin Reed's multi-storeyed men's store in Regent Street, Simpson turned to prominent architect, Joseph Emberton. Like Crabtree at Peter Jones, he looked to the crisp modernism of Erich Mendelsohn to create this tiered façade of alternating bands of Portland stone and metal-framed Crittall windows. The building was crowned by a glascrete canopy that helped to keep the stone stain-free. *The Architect & Building News* said 'it sets a high standard, and we welcome it, not merely for its own merits, but as an object lesson to future rebuilders in Piccadilly.'

Simpson, window display

These are the original non-reflective glass display windows, a device favoured by the London shopfitting firm E Pollard & Co Ltd, using special Pilkington glass. Such windows proved irresistible to young children, and mothers were known to stand their children inside the base so that they could feel the glass for themselves. This distraction, and changing fashions, led to many of these windows being replaced after World War II. The Simpson building was listed in 1970, and this example has therefore been retained.

Simpson, a display of suits

Simeon Simpson, who set up a wholesale tailoring business
in Petticoat Lane in 1894, was always intent that his mass-
produced ready-to-wear garments had the quality of
traditional bespoke tailoring. The DAKS range epitomised this
ideal. After the closure of Simpson in December 1998, DAKS
opened a flagship store in Old Bond Street.

Peter Jones, Sloane Square, exterior view

In 1868, Peter Rees Jones, the son of a Monmouthshire hat manufacturer, opened a draper's shop in Hackney. The business moved to 4–6 Kings Road in 1877. Here the firm prospered, gradually expanding into adjoining buildings. By 1903 Peter Jones had a turnover of £157,000 and employed 300 staff. However, by the time of his death in 1905, the business was in financial difficulty. The following year, John Lewis purchased the company. His son, John Spedan Lewis, took control of Peter Jones in 1916, and it was there in 1920 that he launched the first version of the John Lewis profit-sharing partnership. He oversaw the rebuilding of the store to the designs of William Crabtree and consultants Slater and Moberly. It was constructed in phases between 1932 and 1939, although the Cadogan Gardens/Kings Road corner block was not built until 1964. Crabtree was greatly influenced by the department stores of German architect Erich Mendelsohn, which looked to the simple and efficient style of factory buildings. Crabtree's design was innovative in its use of metal and glass, one of the earliest examples of a non-structural curtain wall. Broken down into vertical strips, the façade seems more like a 1950s office block than a department store.

Peter Jones, ground floor showrooms, the spiral staircase

This stunning corkscrew staircase in steel, with a central tier of glazed display shelves, was based on Mendelsohn's staircase in the De La Warr Pavilion at Bexhill-on-Sea (1935). It is one of the finest architectural features in any London department store.

Peter Jones, the central atrium

Atriums and light wells were a popular feature of department stores, used to entice shoppers upwards through the store and to

light the expansive interiors. By the 1930s, improvements in artificial lighting began to make them less of a necessity. The constructional steelwork of Peter Jones was designed so that they could be floored over to increase retail space. As part of the £100 million refurbishment of the store, due to be completed in 2004, the central atrium has been heightened and escalators inserted into the space to create a grand processional route up through the store.

John Lewis, the front atrium at first floor level

The atrium, here top lit and enhanced with a grid pattern of glazing bars, imbues the crisp, unornamented interior with an aura of grandeur. Unlike the plans for its sister store Peter Jones, the 2001–2 refurbishment of the interiors of John Lewis did not include plans to alter the delightful character of this atrium, which provides shoppers with a seductive view of different departments.

John Lewis, Oxford Street, the Holles Street corner with sculpture by Barbara Hepworth

In 1864 John Lewis opened his first drapery shop in Oxford Street, having previously worked as a buyer at Peter Robinson. For the first six months he operated at a loss, but a bargain purchase of silks is reported to have set the business on a successful footing. His son, John Spedan Lewis, joined the thriving business in 1904 and, after his father's death in 1928, turned the firm into a profit-sharing partnership owned by the employees. The store was badly damaged by bombing in 1940 and much of it was rebuilt in a crisp modern style to the designs of Slater and Moberly. The new store opened on October 17, 1960. The *Winged Figure* by Barbara Hepworth was added to the façade in 1962.

Debenhams, 334–48 Oxford Street, the main entrance

In 1815 William Debenham bought a partnership in a drapery goods store in Wigmore Street. The store became
Debenham & Freebody in the 1850s when William's brother-in-law joined the business. By the end of the 19th century
Debenhams had begun taking over rival retail businesses in London and around the country, and today controls 96 stores.
Debenhams bought Marshall & Snelgrove in 1919, thus acquiring this prime site in Oxford Street. This severe façade, erected
in 1970, is in sharp contrast to the grandeur of nearby Selfridges.

Luxury &
Designer Shops

As the capital of the nation and centre of empire, London
has been a magnet for wealth. The fashionable elite
cherished the luxury items on offer, from bespoke shirts
to fine jewels, and St James's and Mayfair epitomise this
aspect of the city's retail life. In the 18th century these
areas were home to the court and much of the
aristocracy, and thus attracted some of the finest shops.
There were shirt makers and hatters in St James's Street
and Jermyn Street to serve the gentleman who spent
their afternoons in the local clubs. In the Regency period
Bond Street was a place of promenade, while in nearby
Piccadilly there were the fine shops of the Burlington
Arcade. In the 20th century Bond Street continued to be
one of the most famous streets in the world, lined with
art dealers and luxurious jewellery houses like Asprey and
Bentley & Skinner. They were joined by the designer
brands, which became one of the great retail phenomena
of the last decades of the century – movie stars and city
workers alike desired the latest Gucci creation or silver
trinkets from Tiffany. Traditional British names from
Burberry to Turnbull & Asser also call St James's home.
While London has other luxury retail areas, including
Knightsbridge and Sloane Square, Bond Street and its
environs remain the jewel in the crown.

Asprey & Garrard, 165–9 New Bond Street, shopfront and flags

Asprey was founded in 1781, and moved to 166 New Bond Street in 1847, gradually expanding into adjoining houses. The shopfront of 166, enriched with slender barley twist columns, dates from the 1860s, while the rest was added between 1900 and 1926 to match. Garrard is older, dating back to 1721. From the time of Queen Victoria it has been the crown jeweller, responsible for altering the state crown. With the purchase of both firms in the mid 1990s by Prince Jeffri Bolkiah of Brunei, said to be each jeweller's best customer, Garrard's Regent Street showrooms were closed and the businesses were brought together under one roof.

In 2000 the firm was sold and plans were announced to bring back the distinct identities of the two jewellery houses, with Garrard focusing on tiaras, antiques, and fine jewellery. New designers are to be brought in to give Asprey's luxury goods a trendier image. The two firms will have separate premises next door to one another; the new Asprey shop opened at 169 New Bond Street in April 2002.

Asprey & Garrard, fourth-floor workshops, Mr
Geoff Sams working on a special commission

Both Asprey and Garrard have always been known for the
highly skilled craftsmanship that goes into their creations;
throughout the 155 years that Asprey has been in Bond
Street, craftsmen have worked on the premises. The
workshops are a rare survival, and may be some of the
oldest in continuous use on the same site. There are
separate workshops for leather, silver, and jewellery. As well
as stock items, special commissions are also undertaken,
often in the greatest secrecy. Here Mr Geoff Sams,
silversmith, refers to the design drawing during the first
stages of creating a specially commissioned box, probably for
foreign royalty.

Asprey & Garrard,
antique candlesticks

The firm also sells exquisite
antiques, ranging from estate
jewellery and clocks to a fine
selection of first edition and
rare books.

Tessiers, 26 New Bond Street

A favourite of Queen Mary, wife of George V, this firm traces
its roots back to 1817 when Lewis Tessier, the great-
grandson of a French Huguenot immigrant, opened a
jewellery manufacturing business in Soho. By 1852, Tessier
and three of his sons had moved to 26 New Bond Street.
Although they sold the business in the 1880s, their name has
continued as a fixture of Bond Street. The Tessier family had
this wonderful arcaded shopfront erected in 1857. At the
time it was described by *Building News* as being "tawdrily-
painted…the whole of the moulded work…including the
enriched capitals, are a bad imitation of white veined marble,
and the columns are intended to represent Sienna marble.'

Tessiers, interior with Ms Helen Coogan

The interior is lined with fitted mahogany cabinets, gleaming
with jewels and silver. The traditional glass-topped showcase
looks little changed from the Victorian period, with neatly
arranged rows of jewels nestled in velvet-lined boxes. An
antique bronze bust (left) sits majestically below a gas lamp
that would have lit the shop in the late19th century.

Bentley & Skinner, 8 New Bond Street

Bentley & Co was established in 1934 by John Sheldon at 65 New Bond Street. A metallurgist and descendant of Lithuanian jewellers, he had amassed a large collection of gold and antique jewellery after Britain came off the Gold Standard in 1932. A E Skinner, founded in 1881, have been jewellers to the royal family since their appointment by Queen Victoria. Bentley & Co moved to 8 New Bond Street in 1992, and the two firms came together in 1998. Although refronted and remodelled in the mid 19th century, the core of the building probably dates from the 1720s, when this part of Bond Street was first developed. The shopfront, with Corinthian columns flanking the display windows, was designed in 1992, though the grandiose style is similar to that of Tessiers, 26 New Bond Street, built in 1857.

Bentley & Skinner, third floor workshops – Ms Ute Pilditch, pearl stringer, Ms Sarah Griffiths, jeweller, and Mr Graham Simmonds, watchmaker

Since at least the 1750s, 8 New Bond Street has been in use as a shop, home to a hairdresser, cigar importer, court dressmaker, and milliner. For much of that time, the upper storeys were also used as workshops. Such a close relationship between the shop and the workshop is increasingly rare. Bentley & Skinner have continued this tradition, providing space for craftsmen and women, including specialist jewellers as well as the engravers G M Betser & Co, who undertake commissions for Bentley & Skinner and also work freelance.

Bentley & Skinner, the interior

8 New Bond Street is unusual in having a shallow plot, which only allowed for a building one room deep – resonant, however, of the atmosphere of Georgian shops premises which tended to be small, with shop assistants offering goods for inspection from behind a counter. Bentley & Skinner have used this small space to superior effect, creating one of London's most intimate shop interiors, elegantly finished with chandeliers and antique display cabinets.

J W Benson, Hunt & Roskell, and Elizabeth Arden, 25 Old Bond Street, 1923, photograph by Bedford Lemere

The jewellers and silversmiths Hunt & Roskell were established in Bond Street in the early 19th century. In 1866 J W Benson, a watch- and clockmaker from the City, joined the business and this elegant, arcaded shopfront of serpentine marble was added, creating one large shop out of two Georgian terraced houses. By the 1920s, when this photograph was taken, gentleman could shop for baubles downstairs while their wives were pampered by the beauticians at Elizabeth Arden upstairs. These premises are now the home of another famous jeweller, Tiffany, purveyor of gifts to the likes of Victoria Beckham and former *My Fair Lady* star Martine McCutcheon.

Tiffany & Co, 25 Old
Bond Street, looking
north

One of America's most revered institutions, Tiffany was
founded in New York City by Charles Lewis Tiffany and
John B Young in 1837. Starting as a stationery and fancy
goods emporium, by the 1850s it was fast becoming
renowned for its sterling silver creations and jewellery. The
famous stained glass windows and lamps were a later
creation of Charles's son, Louis Comfort Tiffany. Tiffany
opened this lavish flagship store at 25 Old Bond Street in
1986. Their classic 'Tiffany Blue' boxes filled with jewels or
silver trinkets have become a status symbol among
London's style-conscious consumers. They have done little
to change the historic shopfront apart from adding the
American flag and the fine Ormolu clock surmounted by
gilt dolphins. The flags are shown at half-mast to mark the
death of Queen Elizabeth, the Queen Mother in March
2002.

Thomas Goode, 17–22 South Audley Street; Jim Gill, General Manager, welcomes shoppers at the main entrance

Probably the finest shop in London for china and crystal, Thomas Goode retains its Victorian splendour both inside and out. It was established in 1827 when Thomas Goode opened a china business at 15 Mill Street near Hanover Square. In 1845 the business moved to its present site. The premises were rebuilt on a lavish scale to the designs of Ernest George and Peto in two phases in 1875–6 and 1889–91. The Victorian mechanical doors, which open from the pressure of a person stepping on the threshold, are said to be the first example of automatic doors ever built, and are the oldest surviving example still in use.

Thomas Goode, interior

Thomas Goode is known for its lavish displays, and nothing is more indicative of this than the two large ceramic elephants in the windows flanking the mechanical doors. Standing over seven feet tall, they were produced by Minton in collaboration with William Goode and exhibited at the Paris exhibitions of 1878 and 1889. Although they are considered a permanent fixture of the store, they are reported to have a price tag of £5 million.

Thomas Goode, display
of plates

As well as selling every
imaginable brand of china,
from Wedgwood to Versace,
Thomas Goode also
produces its own patterns,
and is known for its bespoke
service. The firm has created
special dinner services for
royalty, presidents, and
celebrities. The showrooms
include a small museum with
examples of their designs.

Thomas Goode, the corridor leading to the gift room

The shop retains much of its Victorian decoration, including hand-painted friezes, stained
glass, and features like this arch painted with cherubs and foliage.

Thomas Goode,
the interior in 1891,
photograph by Bedford
Lemere

The 1875 rebuilding included
a series of top-lit
showrooms, which allowed
glass and china to be
displayed to maximum effect.
This room remains in use
today with only minor
decorative changes.

Thomas Goode,
table display

Partridge Fine Arts, 144–6 New Bond Street, the ground-floor showroom

Bond Street has had links with the fine art trade since the late 18th century when Phillips the auctioneers established their business here. Since then the street has gradually become the centre of London's art and antiques trade, with many galleries and two auction houses nestled in between the designer fashion stores. Partridge is one of the grandest of these establishments, with customers over the firm's 100-year history ranging from billionaire collectors to international museums. Partridge's grand premises were purpose-built in 1912–14 for one of its rivals, the equally famous art dealers Colnaghi, who now have a gallery in Old Bond Street.

Partridge, the picture gallery on the mezzanine floor

This top-lit picture gallery is one of only a few shop spaces in London specially designed for the display of paintings. As well as British and European paintings and decorative arts, Partridge is particularly famous for its collections of French furniture and works of art, which include pieces like the bronze equestrian statue of Louis XV on the table. Partridge is said to have the largest stock of such items for sale outside Paris.

Burberry, 21–3 New Bond Street, the main staircase and displays

Burberry, ground-floor showrooms and handbag displays

This is a perfect example of the modern luxury goods shop interior, which looks back to the 1930s for inspiration. Inlaid wood, leather, and carefully designed lighting are used to display goods in an almost quasi-religious manner. Handbags and dog-coats are presented as precious objects.

Burberry began in 1856, when Thomas Burberry opened an outfitter's shop in Basingstoke, Hampshire. The classic Burberry raincoat, designed at the turn of the century, became regulation clothing during the First World War when it acquired the name 'The Trench Coat'. The camel, black, red, and white check lining was added to the coat in 1924. Since then, the Burberry coat has been one of the most recognisable fashion designs of the 20th century. Its iconic status was assured when Humphrey Bogart wore one in the film *Casablanca*. With the appointment of Rose Marie Bravo as Worldwide Chief Executive in 1997, Burberry has taken the famous coat as a starting point to revamp the brand's image to compete in the expanding international market for luxury goods. At the heart of

this plan was the opening of the new flagship store in New Bond Street. Consisting of 15,000 square feet of retail space over three floors, the shop was designed by English architect Mark Pinney and American interior designer Randall Ridless. Mirroring the new designer collections, the classic Burberry check is used as a theme in the fixtures and fittings of the shop – here it is incorporated into the staircase balustrade and carpeting.

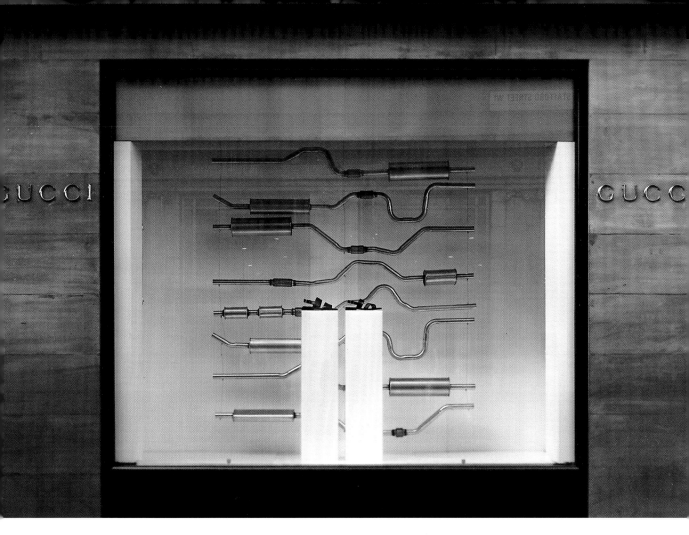

Gucci, 32–3 Old Bond Street, window display

Possibly the most revered of all the luxury brands, this Italian firm was founded in 1921 when Guccio Gucci opened a luggage shop in Florence. By the 1960s Gucci was internationally famous for its handbags and accessories, much favoured by famous personalities like Grace Kelly and Jackie Onassis. Although handbags emblazoned with the firm's classic double G logo are still a cornerstone of the business, in the 1990s Gucci reinvented itself as a fashion house. Designer Tom Ford joined the firm in 1990, and began creating a range of clothes and accessories that have given Gucci a powerful position in the fashion world. This display is a clear example of the power of the Gucci brand: the large window is styled like an art installation, all for the display of a single pair of sandals placed in splendid isolation on pedestals.

Harvie & Hudson, 97 Jermyn Street

One of Jermyn Street's luxury shirtmakers, the long-
established Harvie & Hudson specialises in bespoke shirts. It
has one of the best preserved late-Victorian shopfronts
surviving in the street, with a grand arcade of windows
framed by colourful strips of tiles and sculpted cartouches
above.

Turnbull & Asser, 72 Jermyn Street, the Bury Street façade

A favourite among Wall Street traders, Turnbull & Asser are also shirtmakers to the Prince of Wales and supplied Sean Connery in his role as James Bond. The shop dates to 1903 and has an authentic Edwardian feel, with its carved window surrounds, fanciful cartouches, and rich mahogany interior. It is not an entirely male preserve; their fine shirts, hand-made in Gloucestershire, are also available for women. Female clients include Lauren Bacall. Her American compatriots may account for up to half of the firm's sales these days, and its success is such that a branch has opened in New York.

Lock & Co, Mr James Benning in the doorway, c1880

This early view of Lock & Co, here with a display of top hats, bowlers, and pith helmets, shows that the shopfront has changed little in the last 120 years. In 1850 Lock & Co were commissioned to make the very first bowler hat for their customer, William Coke. The hat was originally designed as a protective hat for riding, and was later mass-produced by the Bowler Brothers, although it is still called a coke hat at Lock & Co. They have made coke hats for Oscar Wilde, Lord Lucan, and possibly the most famous ever, for Charlie Chaplin. Lock made a special metal-rimmed version for the character *Odd Job* in the James Bond film, *Goldfinger*. It was sold by Christie's in 1998 for £55,000. In this photograph, Mr Benning, a partner in the firm, stands in the doorway. It has been suggested that his dress and demeanour may have inspired Lewis Carroll, a customer, to create the character of the *Mad Hatter* in *Alice in Wonderland*.

Lock & Co, 6 St James's Street, the shopfront

One of the oldest shops in continuous use in London, Lock & Co moved to these premises in 1765. The history of the shop can be traced back to 1676, when Robert Davis, hatter, moved his shop from Bishopsgate to St James's Street. His granddaughter, Mary Davis, married a neighbour, James Lock, in 1757, and he took over the business on the death of his father-in-law in 1759. Their descendants continue to run the firm. The shopfront, with a pair of windows and wrought-iron grilles flanking a central entrance, probably dates to the late-Georgian period.

Lock & Co, garret workrooms; Miss Sylvia Fletcher, milliner, finishes a hat

In recent years Lock & Co have added ladies' millinery to their repertoire. Miss Sylvia Fletcher is the chief designer. Favourite of the famous and fashionable, in 1995 she created the hats for Stella McCartney's graduation show at Central St Martin's School of Art and Design. Like artists of yesteryear, Miss Fletcher and her team toil away creating stunning hats in the St James's Street attic.

Lock & Co, ground floor, display of Nelson and Wellington memorabilia

Since the Seven Years War an important facet of Lock's business has been the production of military hats, and the firm supplied both Nelson and Wellington. In the age before sunglasses, Lock fitted a special eye-shade to Nelson's favourite hat after he was partially blinded at the Siege of Calvi, and he wore a Lock hat at Trafalgar. The original designs and a model of the hat are displayed in the shop, as is one of Wellington's plumed hats, similar to that worn at Waterloo. Lock have also undertaken royal commissions – they used the wooden template on the left to ensure that both the State and Imperial crowns were a comfortable fit for the Queen at her coronation in 1953.

Lock & Co, ground floor showrooms; Mr Patrick Lamb and Mr Brian Towers demonstrate the conformateur

This head-measuring device, called a conformateur, has been used to fit all bespoke and hard hats for the last 150 years. It maps the contour of the head on a piece of card to 1/6 actual scale. This is then used to ensure that a hat is moulded to a perfect fit. The cards are kept for future commissions – those of famous customers, from Charlie Chaplin and Charles de Gaulle to Mike Tyson, are displayed in the shop. The conformateur has recently been used as a measuring tool by a French doctor who treats children with malformed skulls.

John Lobb, 9 St James's Street, general view of shopfront

Established in 1849, John Lobb had a shop in Regent Street from the 1860s and opened a branch in St James's Street in the 1890s, where the firm has occupied various premises ever since. It continues as a family-run business, creating meticulously constructed shoes. Clients, who have included Queen Victoria, Cecil Beaton, and Frank Sinatra, must be prepared to wait many months for shoes guaranteed to be a perfect fit. This delightful shopfront, with its lamp decorated with a boot, dates from after World War II. Within the ground-floor showroom and basement are elaborate workshops where clients can watch Lobb's skilled shoemakers at work.

John Lobb, lasts and the last warehouse

Making shoes at Lobb is a complicated business. Clients must first be measured, with individual features of each foot noted, and tracings of the feet made. These are used by the last-maker, who carves wooden models, called lasts, which are then used to construct the shoes. Thousands of lasts are kept in the shop's basement workshops, and are altered when necessary to ensure that clients receive perfectly fitting and comfortable shoes. The lasts of deceased famous customers, including those of Jackie Onassis and Emperor Haile Selassi of Ethiopia, shown above, are kept for posterity.

John Lobb, Mr Stephen Pavely boning up a boot

A pair of Lobb shoes make their way through the hands of various craftsmen, each with a specific skill. A clicker cuts the eight individual pieces of leather necessary to create the upper of the shoe. These are then stiffened, lined, shaped, and sewn together by the closer, while the sole and heal are added by the maker. Finally the polisher brings the leather to a fine sheen. Here a boot is being polished with an animal bone that helps flatten the grain of the leather. The entire process can take as long as eight months and the final product can cost upwards of £1400.

James Purdey & Sons, 57–8 South Audley Street, the entrance

The grand Mayfair premises of Purdey are crowned by an elaborate royal arms above pink granite columns flanking the entrance. Gunmakers since 1814, they have had a long association with the royal family; Queen Victoria made her first purchase from the firm in 1838. Originally situated in Oxford Street, the firm moved to this specially built shop in 1881. Guns were once handmade in workshops in the basement, but the workshops have now moved to Hammersmith.

James Purdey & Sons, Mr Robin Nathan holding a
20 bore side-by-side game gun

For almost two centuries Purdey & Sons have been making
guns for sportsmen who enjoy such country pursuits as
hunting and shooting. Its expertly crafted guns were also
essential kit for big game hunters and explorers who
charted the vast wilderness ranges of Britain's former
empire. The shop's interior is decorated with photographs
and memorabilia, including animal trophies donated by
customers. These recall an age, before the advent of wildlife
protection, when a safari was often a dangerous and difficult
trek into harsh terrain.

James Purdey & Sons, gun display

Purdey's ledgers date back to 1816, giving details of every
individually numbered gun. Customers are usually measured
and guns made to their specifications. Where once it was
European monarchs and aristocracy, today it is wealthy
Americans who account for many of Purdey's sales. Guns
and rifles can take up to two years to make, with hundreds
of hours of craftsmanship going into each one. Stocks are
carved from Turkish walnut, and finishing details include finely
engraved metalwork in silver or gold, sometimes with
miniature landscape scenes filled with birds or game. Such
time and craftsmanship is not cheap, and a pair of shotguns
can cost over £90,000 depending on the bore size and
detailing.

Food Shops and Grocery Stores

London's ever growing population has always ensured a constant array of butchers, grocers, fishmongers, bakers, and wine merchants, spread across the capital's neighbourhoods. Initially some would have occupied simple, open-fronted shops, with produce displayed on tiered counters or from hooks. Examples of this way of selling are still to be found. During the Victorian period, food shops could be as extravagantly designed as other types of shops. Butchers' and fishmongers' shops were lined with finely decorated tiles for obvious reasons of cleanliness and also for visual appeal. Provision dealers offered Londoners not only the finest British produce but also exotic delicacies imported from around the world. The rise of supermarkets after World War II put many grocers and provision shops out of business but, despite their size, supermarkets have never been able to fully satisfy the eclectic tastes of London's cosmopolitan population. From the oldest wine merchant in the world to organic grocers and ethnic delis, London's smaller food shops are a much-loved feature of the metropolis.

Berry Bros & Rudd, 3 St James's Street, shopfront

Nestled in the shadow of Henry VIII's great palace of St James's, Berry Bros are one of the oldest wine merchants in the world. They can trace their origins back to 1698, when the Widow Bourne set up a grocer's business on this site. The coffee mill sign hanging at the far left is a reminder of this early history, when the shop supplied coffee and tea to the local coffee houses. The business came to specialise solely in wine in the early 1800s, a half century after one of the widow's descendants had married into the Berry family. The firm continues to be family owned. Part of the magnificent arcaded shopfront probably dates from the late 18th century; the right window and entrance door are original, while the other three windows, based on an early 19th-century drawing in the firm's archives, were part of a restoration undertaken in 1931.

Berry Bros & Rudd, the ground-floor shop premises

In the 1730s the Widow Bourne's son-in-law, William Pickering, rebuilt the house and the shop. The apparently little changed interior of the shop, with its bare, uneven floorboards and oak panelled walls, gives the customer the impression of stepping back into the 18th century. However, over the centuries, interior fittings have been altered and walls moved to enlarge the space. From 1765 the old coffee scales (right) were used to weigh famous customers – from the Prince Regent and Beau Brummell to the Duke of Wellington and Napoleon III. Lord Byron was supposedly so obsessed with his weight that he had himself weighed with and without his boots on. In more recent times, Laurence Olivier, Evelyn Waugh, and the Aga Khan III took to the scales, all having their weights entered in red leather-bound ledgers.

Berry Bros & Rudd,
the south-east corner of
the shop

Berry's premises are more museum than shop, with displays consisting of antique wine bottles and memorabilia associated with the history of the firm, or with wine and wine making. The firm's vast stocks of wine and spirits are stored in underground vaults and in temperature-controlled warehouses located at Basingstoke. The royal arms over the fireplace are a reminder of Berry's long association with the British royal family, whom they have supplied since the reign of George III. Today they hold warrants from the Queen and the Prince of Wales.

Berry Bros & Rudd, the basement cellars and cellar dining room

Parts of these cellars, which run under St James's Street and Pall Mall, date back to Tudor times, and legend has it that they were once linked by a door to St James's Palace. With a total area of approximately 8000 square feet, they are the largest working cellars in the capital, with storage space for 100,000 bottles. The directors' reserves kept here are valued at over £1 million. Parts of the cellars were used as a secret meeting place by Prince Louis Napoleon (later Emperor Napoleon III of France) and his supporters in the 1840s, as they planned his return to France. Today a dining room is used for wine tasting and private functions.

R Twining & Co, 216 the Strand, shopfront decoration

Said to be the oldest shop run from the same site and by the same family, Twinings opened in 1706 as a coffee house serving tea, coffee, brandy, and spa waters at the sign of the golden lion in the Strand. The growing popularity of tea drinking led the founder, Thomas Twining, to focus his business entirely on the tea trade, and he was soon supplying London's aristocratic elite with many varieties of the much-coveted drink. The narrow façade is said to be the smallest shopfront in London. Tradition has it that it was built in 1787 by Thomas's grandson Richard, who incorporated the old golden lion sign above the door and added the two Chinese figures either side as a reminder of the origins of tea.

Allen & Co, Mr Bob O'Dwyer with racks of lamb

Allen & Co, 117 Mount Street

117–21 Mount Street was designed by the architect James Trant Smith, and constructed in 1886–7 as part of a rebuilding programme undertaken by the Duke of Westminster's Grosvenor Estate. Smith's richly decorated terracotta and red brick façade was described by the Duke as 'overdone and wanting in simplicity'. This corner shop was occupied by butcher Edgar Green, who had been a tenant in the street before rebuilding. He was given special permission to hang carcasses outside his shop by the Duke of Westminster himself.

Allen & Co, a long established Mayfair butchers, succeeded Green after his death in the 1890s. They have continued the practice of hanging carcasses outside and in the windows. Allen's are proud of their friendly service and quality meat – some customers have been visiting the shop since before World War II. No cellophane-wrapped chops are to be found here. Meat is cut to your order right in front of you, goods are weighed, and the butcher tells the cashier what you are to pay. This shop supplies not only private individuals but also some of London's most famous restaurants, hotels, and clubs; Jamie Oliver used the shop in his *Naked Chef* programme.

W Plumb, detail of tiling

W Plumb, 493 Hornsey Road, Islington, counter and hanging rails

From the Victorian period butchers' shops were traditionally fitted with tiles to keep interiors cool and easy to clean. However, very few in London were as grandly decorated as this example in Islington. Brightly coloured art nouveau tiles decorate the walls and the interiors are finished with mosaic tiles, mahogany fittings, and fine marble counter tops. One of London's most exquisite shop interiors, it is sadly no longer in use.

Cows and sheep graze in an ideal landscape, in a decorative scene once commonplace in London's butchers' shops. This delightful pastoral scene contrasts starkly with the reality of the butcher's trade, which involved preparing the meat on the marble counters above this tile panel.

Paxton & Whitfield, 93 Jermyn Street, the cheese counter

Paxton & Whitfield have been tingling the tastebuds of Jermyn Street shoppers since 1835. The partnership was founded in 1797, and the firm traces itself back still further to a modest cheese stall set up by one Stephen Callum at Clare Market, near Aldwych in 1742. Winston Churchill believed it was the best cheese shop in London, and modern shoppers are equally impressed by its vast selection, with some 300 varieties from all over the world. With a particular emphasis on cheeses of the British Isles, Paxton & Whitfield show that Britain's cheese industry is just as formidable as that of the French.

Paxton & Whitfield, window display

A selection of breads, preserves, and wine in the shop's large windows tantalise Jermyn Street shoppers. It is the perfect place to stock up for a summer picnic in nearby St James's Park.

Charbonnel et Walker, 1 Royal Arcade

Beautifully wrapped chocolate bars adorn the window to entice shoppers who stroll through the arcade. This famous chocolatier has been in business since 1875, when the then Prince of Wales (later Edward VII) encouraged Mme Charbonnel of Maison Boissier chocolatiers in Paris to come to London, where she joined forces with Mrs Walker and opened a shop in New Bond Street. They moved to the Royal Arcade in the 1970s. The firm is still popular with the royal family, holding a warrant from the Queen. Ellen Terry, Noel Coward, and John Gielgud are among the many famous customers who have enjoyed their hand-made chocolates.

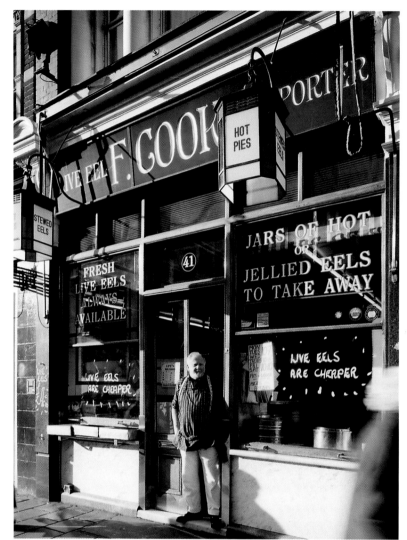

F Cooke, live eels

One of London's most notorious dishes, eels could be purchased live from Cooke's where they were stored in specially made metal trays. At one time Cooke's was one of London's foremost eel wholesalers.

F Cooke, Eel, Pie and Mash Shop, 41 Kingsland High Street, Hackney; Fred Cooke stands in the doorway

The Cooke family have been selling pies and eels since at least 1865. Over the years the business has steadily grown to include shops in Hackney, Bermondsey, Hoxton, and Clerkenwell. This branch was opened in 1910. Lavishly accented with marble and stained glass lamps, the windows opened to allow passers-by to buy eels and pies from the street. To the rear of the shop there was a bakery and a restaurant with skylights, the walls decorated with Art Nouveau tiles. Although the shop closed in 1997, it remains intact and is home to a Chinese restaurant.

James Knight of Mayfair Ltd, 8 Shepherd Market

Once the haunt of prostitutes and villains, this part of Mayfair is now a delightful enclave of stylish shops and cafes. Grafted onto an 18th-century terrace house, this fishmonger's and poulterer's shop is a combination of periods and styles. Regency-style pilaster strips flank the windows while the iron grille above looks to the Gothic revival popularised by the Victorians. The playful shellfish motifs in the tiling allude to the shop's function. These were probably a 20th-century addition, along with the finely carved Prince of Wales feathers, which denote that Knight supplies the Prince of Wales's household.

L S Mash & Sons, 11 Atlantic Road, Brixton; left to right:
Mr Lorne Mash, Mr Daniel Murphy and Mr Ian Ridley

One of many shops situated in the railway arches around Brixton Station, this fishmongers'
was opened in 1934 by a Mr Mills. Mr Lorne Mash began work for Mr Mills at the age of 14,
and eventually inherited the business. The firm is now run by his son, Lorne. A metal grill
crowns this open-fronted shop, decorated with marvellous sculptures of various types of fish.

J Evans, 35 Conway Street, Euston

Now a private residence, this was once a shop providing the locality with milk and other dairy products. The shopfront, with blue and white glazed tiles and glass fascia, dates to the early 20th century. London's small dairies gradually lost market share to the large provision shops that became popular at the end of the 19th century, and many died out altogether with the arrival of supermarkets in the mid 20th century. However, J Evans was unusual in that it continued in business into the 1980s.

Fruits of Paradise, 79
The Broadway, Southall

A traditional open-fronted
fruit and vegetable stand,
with the retail area extended
into the street by the use of
the awning. Like the
neighbouring bazaars, the
display of goods dominates
the architectural space.

Kennedy's, 64 and 66 Deptford High Street, view
through the window

Kennedy's is part of a south London chain of butchers and
provision shops established in 1877. The ordered display of
meat, pies, and canned goods is accentuated with signs
advertising both the firm's history and its specialities.

Crackerjack Supermarket and Off-Licence,
56–64 Peckham High Street; Mr Singh in his shop

In the last 30 years London's Asian community has done
more to reinvigorate the retail prospects of the capital's local
high streets than any other immigrant group. They opened
corner shops, newsagents, and cash and carry businesses in
the often-deprived areas where they settled, and stayed
open for long hours, a godsend to a late-working populace.
Their success helped to encourage other businesses back to
inner-city communities, creating vibrancy where once there
was only decline. The Crackerjack in Peckham is a classic
example of the local shop – piled floor to ceiling with goods
sold at discount prices, with the odd exotic item, like Kama
Sutra beer (left), adding a bit of zest.

A Gold, Mrs Safia Thomas behind the counter
of her shop

The shop owners, Mr & Mrs Thomas, considered the history
of their premises and the Spitalfields area when designing
their shop interior. Traditional materials and styling, like the
carved wood shelving behind the counter, are combined
with artfully arranged displays of goods to create an old
world charm. The classic Walls Bacon advertisement (right)
and telephone (centre) add to the overall atmosphere.

A Gold, 42 Brushfield Street, Spitalfields

This simple late Victorian shop opposite Spitalfields Market
has been home to various businesses in the last 150 years,
including a milliner, a boot maker, and a coffee house. The
present owners took inspiration from a former tenant, A
Gold, French Milliner, whose sign still appears on the shop
fascia, to name their speciality food shop. Concentrating on
traditional British produce, this shop is an example of the
successful regeneration of the area in recent years.

Sainsbury's, Greenwich Peninsula Branch, main entrance

In 1869 John and Mary Sainsbury opened a small dairy shop in Drury Lane. By 1900 they had 48 shops in London and the South East selling a variety of provisions, poultry, dairy, and meat products. The early branches were all counter service shops, and their first self-service supermarket, in Croydon, was not opened until 1950. Although in recent years they have suffered fierce competition from rival Tescos, Sainsbury's continues to be one of Britain's best-known brand names. The Greenwich superstore was opened in 1999 as part of a regeneration scheme for the brownfield sites surrounding the Millennium Dome. Described as the first eco-superstore for its innovative construction, the structure is partially buried under earth. While it may look bizarre, this makes it 50% more energy efficient than the normal supermarket.

Sainsbury's, windmill and solar panels (left); woodland planting at the rear of the store (right)

In keeping with the eco-friendly nature of the whole design, the exterior signage and lighting are powered by windmills and solar panels set on poles within the car park. Although the car park seems to contradict the ecological concept, there are a number of charging bays for electric cars. Around the back of the store a nature reserve in miniature has been created in association with The Woodland Trust. This is intended to be an educational tool for local schools and also fulfils a practical function, with the reed beds cleansing run-off water from the store's service yard, which is then collected in a small lagoon.

Sainsbury's, the checkout counters

The mosaic tiles and mahogany fittings that were once the standard for all Sainsbury's shops seem a distant memory in this modern environment. In terms of lighting, however, the design recalls John Sainsbury's dying words in 1928: 'Keep the shops well lit'. The store is almost entirely lit naturally from above by the beautifully arched and cleverly designed roof. Halogen lighting is used sparingly for product display and in a thin strip above the cash registers, and an ambient lighting system switches on automatically when it becomes too dark.

Sainsbury's, the centre aisle

Here the store is decked out for Christmas 2000. The space is well organised, with aisles shortened and widened for greater manoeuvrability, bringing it closer to the more convenient and spacious American model. It also has one of the largest product ranges of any branch, and includes an in-store pharmacy, bakery, meat counter, fish counter, deli, and Starbucks Coffee shop.

Select Bibliography

Adburgham, Alison *Shopping in style: London from the Restoration to Edwardian elegance*, London, Thames & Hudson, 1979

Adburgham, Alison *Shops and shopping 1800–1914*, London, Barrie & Jenkins, 1989

Arnold, Sue *A tale of curds and whey: a short history of Paxton & Whitfield*, 1997

B, H J *Burlington Arcade: Being a discourse on shopping for the elite*, London, The Favil Press, 1925

Bayne-Powell, Rosamond *Eighteenth century London Life*, London, John Murray, 1937

Calladine, Tony A paragon of lucidity and taste: the Peter Jones department store, *Transactions of the Ancient Monuments Society*, 45, 2001, 7–27

Calloway, Stephen (ed) *The House of Liberty: masters of style and decoration*, London, Thames & Hudson, 1992

Campbell, R *The London tradesman*, London, 1747

Clunn, Chris *Eels, pie and mash*, London, Museum of London, 1995

Collins' *Guide to London and neighbourhood*, London, William Collins, 1880

Cruickshank, Dan Reinforcing Classicism, *Architects' Journal*, 195, 1992, 22–33

Dale, Tim *Harrods: a palace in Knightsbridge*, London, Harrods, 1995

Davis, Dorothy *A history of shopping*, London, Routledge & Kegan Paul, 1966

Day-Lewis, Tamasin While Selfridges swept, *Vanity Fair*, 477, May 2000, 100–5

Dean, David *English shop fronts from contemporary source books 1792–1840*, London, Alec Tiranti, 1970

Desebrock, Jean *The book of Bond Street old and new*, London, Tallis Press, 1978

Ferry, John William *A history of the department store*, New York, The Macmillan Company, 1960

Geist, Johann Friedrich *Arcades: The history of a building type*, Massachusetts, MIT Press, 1985

Harwood, Elain and Saint, Andrew *London* (Exploring England's Heritage series), London, HMSO, 1991

Hatchards 1797–1997, London, Hatchards, 1997

Hobhouse, Hermione *A history of Regent Street*, London, Macdonald and Jane's and Queen Anne Press, 1975

Honeycombe, Gordon *Selfridges seventy-five years: The story of the store 1909–1984*, London, Park Lane Press, 1984

Inwood, Stephen *A history of London*, London, Macmillan, 1998

Kershman, Andrew and Ireson, Ally *The London market guide*, London, Metro Publications, 2000

MacKeith, Margaret *The history and conservation of shopping arcades*, London, Mansell, 1986

MacKeith, Margaret *Shopping arcades 1817–1939: A gazetteer of extant British arcades*, London, Mansell, 1985

Malcolm, James Peller *Anecdotes of the manners and customs of London in the eighteenth century*, London, Longman, Hurst, Rees and Orme, 1808

McKendrick, Neil, Brewer, John and Plumb, J H *The birth of a consumer society: The commercialisation of eighteenth-century England*, London, Europa, 1982

Mingey, G E *Georgian London*, London, BT Batsford, 1975

Morrison, Kathryn *A nation of shoppers: the history of retail buildings in England*, London, Yale University Press, forthcoming 2003

Moss, Michael and Turton, Alison *A legend of retailing House of Fraser*, London,

Weidenfeld & Nicolson, 1989

Murray, Venetia *High society in the Regency period*, London, Penguin, 1998

Powers, Alan *Shop fronts*, London, Chatto & Windus, 1989

Prestlove, James Stock of ages, *Time Out*, 4–11 August 1999, no 1511, 31–6

Rappaport, Erika Diane *Shopping for pleasure: Women in the making of London's West End*, Princeton, Princeton University Press, 2000

Rudé, George *Hanoverian London 1714–1808*, London, Secker & Warburg, 1971

Survey of London, XXVII *Spitalfields and Mile End New Town*, 1957

Survey of London, XXIX–XXX *Parish of St James, Westminster, Part I: South of Piccadilly*, 1960

Survey of London, XXXVI *The Parish of St Paul Covent Garden*, 1970

Survey of London, XL *The Grosvenor Estate in Mayfair*, 1980

Survey of London, XLI *South Kensington: Brompton*, 1983

Survey of London, XLII *South Kensington: Kensington Square to Earl's Court*, 1986

Survey of London, XLV *Knightsbridge*, 2000

The delectable history of Fortnum & Mason, London, Fortnum & Mason, nd

Weinreb, Ben and Hibbert, Christopher (eds) *The London Encyclopaedia*, London, Macmillan, 1983

Whitbourn, Frank *Mr Lock of St James's Street*, London, Heinemann, 1971

Wurman, Richard Saul *London Access*, New York, Access Press (Harper Perennial), 1993